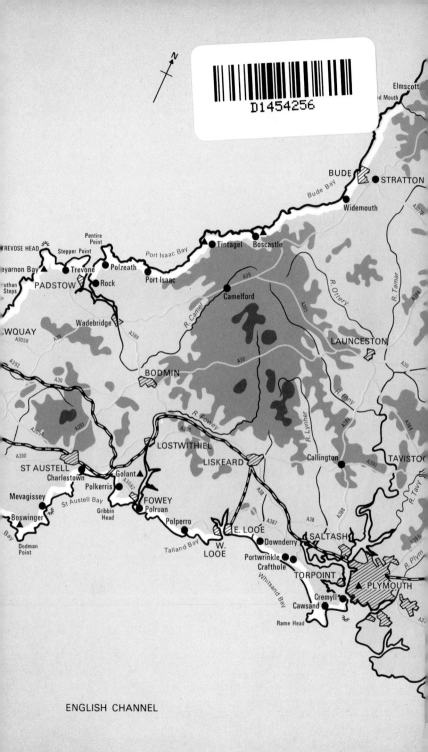

Cliffs at Bude

Cornwall Coast Path

Section 3 of the South-West Peninsula Coast Path

Edward C. Pyatt

Long-Distance Footpath Guide No 5

London Her Majesty's Stationery Office

Published for the Countryside Commission

Front cover:
Rocks at Land's End

Back cover:
Ancient mine workings

Inside back cover:
Land's End

The maps in this guide are extracts from Ordnance Survey maps
1:50,000 (approximately 1¼ in. to the mile) and have been prepared
from O.S. Sheets 180, 190, 200, 201, 203, 204

Drawings by Paul Sharp
Nature drawings by Harry Titcombe

Government bookshops
49 High Holborn, London WC1V 6HB
13a Castle Street, Edinburgh EH2 3AR
41 The Hayes, Cardiff CF1 1JW
Brazennose Street, Manchester M60 8AS
Southey House, Wine Street, Bristol BS1 2BQ
258 Broad Street, Birmingham B1 2HE
80 Chichester Street, Belfast BT1 4JY
Government publications are also available through booksellers

Prepared for the Countryside Commission by the
Central Office of Information, 1975

Long-Distance Footpath Guides published for the Countryside
Commission by HMSO:
The Pennine Way, by Tom Stephenson: 120 pages, £2·50 net
The Cleveland Way, by Alan Falconer: 144 pages, £1·80 net
The Pembrokeshire Coast Path, by John H. Barrett: 124 pages,
£2·50 net
Offa's Dyke Path, by John B. Jones: 124 pages, £2·50 net

In preparation:
Ridgeway Path
South Downs Way

Other sections of the South-West Peninsula Coast Path will be
published later. They are: Section 1, Dorset; Section 2, South
Devon; Section 4, Somerset and North Devon

Countryside Commission, John Dower House,
Crescent Place, Cheltenham, Glos. GL50 3RA

Printed in England for Her Majesty's Stationery Office by
W. S. Cowell Ltd., Ipswich, Suffolk

 ISBN 0 11 700740 4   Dd 288812 Pro 3867 K120 5/76

Maps of Route

The waymark sign is
used in plaque or stencil
form by the Countryside
Commission on long-distance footpaths

Maps reference

ROADS AND PATHS

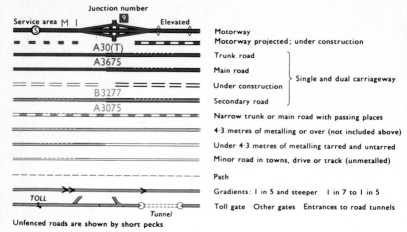

Junction number

Service area M I   9   Elevated

A30(T)

A3675

B3277

A3075

TOLL

Tunnel

Motorway
Motorway projected; under construction

Trunk road

Main road

Under construction

Secondary road

Single and dual carriageway

Narrow trunk or main road with passing places

4·3 metres of metalling or over (not included above)

Under 4·3 metres of metalling tarred and untarred

Minor road in towns, drive or track (unmetalled)

Path

Gradients: 1 in 5 and steeper   1 in 7 to 1 in 5

Toll gate   Other gates   Entrances to road tunnels

Unfenced roads are shown by short pecks

PUBLIC RIGHTS OF WAY

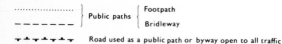

Public paths { Footpath / Bridleway

Road used as a public path or byway open to all traffic

Public rights of way indicated by these symbols have been derived from Definitive Maps as amended by later enactments or instruments held by Ordnance Survey on 1st December 1972, and are shown subject to the limitations imposed by the scale of mapping

The representation on this map of any other road, track or path is no evidence of the existence of a right of way

RAILWAYS

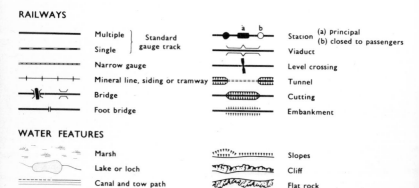

Multiple } Standard gauge track

Single

Narrow gauge

Mineral line, siding or tramway

Bridge

Foot bridge

Station (a) principal / (b) closed to passengers

Viaduct

Level crossing

Tunnel

Cutting

Embankment

WATER FEATURES

Marsh

Lake or loch

Canal and tow path

Aqueduct

Ferry foot

Ferry vehicle

Foot bridge

Light vessel, lighthouse and beacon

Slopes

Cliff

Flat rock

Sand and mud

Sand and shingle

Low water mark

High water mark

Highest point to which tides flow

vi

GENERAL FEATURES

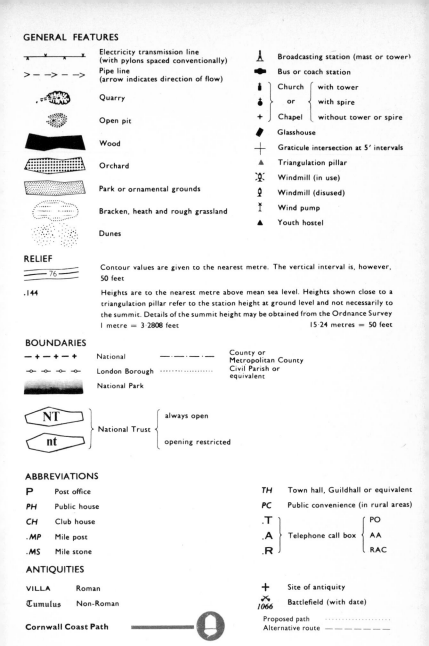

Electricity transmission line
(with pylons spaced conventionally)

Pipe line
(arrow indicates direction of flow)

Quarry

Open pit

Wood

Orchard

Park or ornamental grounds

Bracken, heath and rough grassland

Dunes

Broadcasting station (mast or tower)

Bus or coach station

Church { with tower
or { with spire
Chapel { without tower or spire

Glasshouse

Graticule intersection at 5' intervals

Triangulation pillar

Windmill (in use)

Windmill (disused)

Wind pump

Youth hostel

RELIEF

—— 76 ——
Contour values are given to the nearest metre. The vertical interval is, however, 50 feet

.144
Heights are to the nearest metre above mean sea level. Heights shown close to a triangulation pillar refer to the station height at ground level and not necessarily to the summit. Details of the summit height may be obtained from the Ordnance Survey

1 metre = 3·2808 feet   15·24 metres = 50 feet

BOUNDARIES

— + — + — +   National

-o- -o- -o- -o-   London Borough

National Park

— · — · — · —   County or Metropolitan County

··················   Civil Parish or equivalent

NT } National Trust { always open

nt } { opening restricted

ABBREVIATIONS

P   Post office
PH   Public house
CH   Club house
.MP   Mile post
.MS   Mile stone

TH   Town hall, Guildhall or equivalent
PC   Public convenience (in rural areas)
.T ⎫
.A ⎬ Telephone call box { PO
.R ⎭   { AA
                        { RAC

ANTIQUITIES

VILLA   Roman
Tumulus   Non-Roman

Cornwall Coast Path

+   Site of antiquity
⚔ 1066   Battlefield (with date)

Proposed path   ··················
Alternative route   — — — — — —

Inter–visibility

The distance of the visible horizon (D miles) can be calculated from the height of the viewpoint (H metres) using the following empirical formula:

$$D = 2·4 \sqrt{H}$$

(assuming an average value for vertical variation of refraction in the latitude of England).
To decide whether two objects are inter-visible, on a line of sight passing over the sea, we work out the distance of the visible horizon from each. If these two distances added together are less than the distance between the two places measured on the map, then one cannot be seen from the other.

Introduction

The Cornwall Coast Path is the central portion of the projected 515-mile South-West Peninsula Coast Path, which will eventually extend with rights of way from Minehead in Somerset to South Haven Point beside Poole Harbour in Dorset. The walker enters Cornwall in the north by a small plank footbridge across the little stream at Marsland Mouth in the wild country between Bude and Hartland Point and leaves it 268 miles later by a ferry across the deep channel between the Hamoaze and Plymouth Sound. This is the mouth of the River Tamar which, rising only four miles west of the start of the path, serves, for most of its length, to divide Cornwall from Devon.

After the second world war there was a resurgence of feeling about access to and preservation of the British countryside, which led the Minister of Town and Country Planning to call for a comprehensive report. The result was the now famous *National Parks of England and Wales*, by John Dower, which foreshadowed the many innovations and developments of subsequent years. His recommendations included the setting up of "footpaths and bridleways, with signposts, stiles, gates and bridges . . .". "I found", he said of the Cornish coast, "long stretches of 'coastguards' path' still plain on the ground . . . and I could see no reason why all should not readily be linked up again with continuous public rights of way."

A National Parks Committee was set up which, reporting in 1947, recommended "continuous cliff-edge routes generally following the line of the old coastguards' path. . . . Indeed a coastal path by cliff, bay, dune, beach and estuary, round the whole of England and Wales . . . is not beyond conception." The matter was developed in more detail by a secondary committee under Sir Arthur Hobhouse, which devoted itself entirely to questions of footpaths and access. Reporting later the same year, the committee endorsed the earlier recommendations and put forward more detailed suggestions for specific coast paths, including those of Cornwall.

In 1949 the National Parks and Access to the Countryside Act set up the National Parks Commission and detailed work was begun on a number of long-distance routes. Proposals for a Cornwall North Coast Path of 135 miles were submitted and approved in 1952, and for a Cornwall South Coast Path of 133 miles in 1953-54. Negotiations with landowners were protracted, and it was not until 19 May 1973 that the two paths were opened as the Cornwall Coast Path.

Cliff-top pathways such as this cannot readily be compared with long-distance inland routes like the Pennine Way. Here we aim to 1

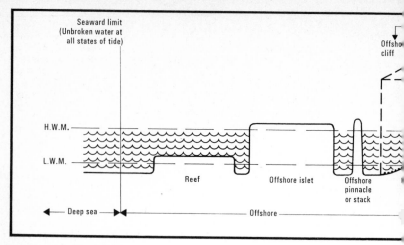

Definition of coastline features

hug the sea's edge as closely as difficulties of terrain or problems of private ownership will permit, a guiding principle which makes it difficult for the walker to lose the way to any appreciable extent. Almost everywhere a diversion inland leads in under a mile to roads or cart-tracks and so to habitations and people; indeed the path, in its windings, crosses or touches on roads and tracks at frequent intervals. Unlike travel among hills or mountains, tantamount to venturing into an alien environment, here, while skirting an environment that is even more alien—the sea—one is never out of contact with familiar lowland terrain. One is able to study the moods and vagaries of the sea from a position of safety on the cliff top. These moods may be both impressive and ferocious but the walker can turn his back on them at his leisure, he is not directly involved and does not have to battle his way. out of a precarious situation. Furnished with 1:50,000 O.S. map and compass, guided by waymarks and signposts, he has little excuse for being lost, except perhaps on an occasional short stretch. Even in a mist he can use his compass and turn inland.

Waymarking, whether by wooden signpost, concrete plinth or the stylised "acorn" of the Countryside Commission, should eventually solve all one's route-finding problems. Difficulties may arise from the necessity of escaping from time to time from inhabited places on to the next cliff. Estates of new houses, caravan parks and chalet villages may block the way. Which is the new road to follow in order to reach some stile and footpath, hidden away behind them? Or the walker may be nonplussed by a streamlet across his path, flowing in a dense belt of shrubs. The path fades out, where does it enter the shrubbery? Choose wrongly and you are faced with time-consuming and temper-trying bush-whacking.

Ups and downs alternate more rapidly than in mountains. One is sometimes on the cliff top looking out over miles of seascape on the one hand and expanses of landscape on the other. Soon one finds oneself at sea level—a beach or cove at the foot of high cliffs—experi-

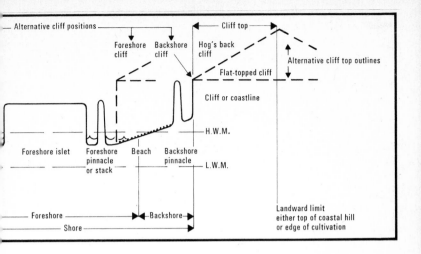

Alternative cliff positions — Cliff top

Foreshore cliff | Backshore cliff | Hog's back cliff

Alternative cliff top outlines

Flat-topped cliff

Cliff or coastline

H.W.M.

Foreshore islet | Foreshore pinnacle or stack | Beach | Backshore pinnacle

L.W.M.

Foreshore — Backshore

Shore

Landward limit either top of coastal hill or edge of cultivation

encing with Richard Jefferies, that "the sea seems higher than the spot where I stand, its surface on a higher level—raised like a green mound—as if it would burst in and occupy the space up to the foot of the cliff in a moment".

In these contiguous yet widely diverse environments the walker experiences a broad spectrum of seashore life, of bird and plant life appropriate to sea-cliffs, estuaries, dunes, hill tops and moorlands. Ancient man fled to and fortified many a promontory to escape from his fellows. He left behind too burial places, stone circles, villages and other sites whose purpose we can no longer fathom. Later man built harbours and sea walls, lighthouses and daymarks, mined and quarried the land and finally came to use it as a holiday recreation centre. All these things, and many more, are to be seen as we pass along.

The walker on the path will usually come by car and thus be forced to return to his starting point at the end of the day. The use of two cars, or of local transport facilities, enable continuous walks to be undertaken, but it is only the "on-and-on" walker who experiences all that the path has to offer, and indeed this is the method to be recommended.

Where is the walker to sleep? This is happy country indeed for the "bed and breakfast" traveller—there is so much of this type of accommodation along the coast, that he will experience little difficulty, except perhaps in school holidays, when turning up unbooked, in securing reasonable overnight lodgings. The lightweight camper is not so well served. He has to use camp sites or ask permission to pitch his tent; he is excluded from pitching on National Trust property and alongside the right of way of the path. An added disadvantage is the considerably greater load of equipment he must carry in order to achieve his freedom. Yet in the cool of the morning or the evening, when the holiday crowds are indoors sleeping or eating, he will be at one with nature in a way they can never know about. Lastly comes 3 what is called "sleeping rough", though it is hard to understand why as the bivouacker needs equipment more sophisticated and therefore more expensive than the camper does. Leaving no signs of his presence or of his passing, the bivouacker has everything in his favour except one—how to get his drinking water, because natural water in an area so densely populated must always be suspect.

The diagram (pages 2–3) illustrates the main features of a cliff coastline such as are met along the way. The existence of a backshore beach implies that the walker has an alternative line at the cliff foot, if the rock is not unduly friable. Even if the beach is only foreshore, that is, exposed for only a part of each tide, it is still available as an alternative route provided suitable care is taken. Such beaches should be tackled only on a falling tide; the walker must keep an eye open for easy ways up the cliff and be prepared to turn back in plenty of time. The maximum tidal range everywhere on this coast is 16 feet, which gives some idea of how high one has to climb to escape the clutches of the sea.

There is no call to recommend a technique for walking, nor is it necessary to offer stern advice about equipment. The walker intent on covering long distances will carry as little as possible. He will already have favourite lightweight garments to counter rain, wind and hot sunshine, all of which will be met at some time or other. He safeguards his feet, possibly by carrying two differing pairs of foot-gear, such as stout vibram-soled shoes and tennis shoes with a springy instep, thus prepared for whatever terrain is likely to be encountered; the contrast in footwear also helps to spin out the miles. Sandals and high heels are not suitable; fell or climbing boots are not necessary. Long trousers are to be preferred to shorts for negotiating the narrow paths through often dense vegetation.

Walking the path has no rules, apart from consideration for one's fellows and for the amenities of the environment. It enables the walker to escape from motor roads into secluded country. Our continued vigilance is needed to ensure that it remains to serve us in just this way in the future.

Marsland Mouth to Port Isaac

40 miles

The north coast of Cornwall consists basically of two huge bays facing roughly north-west. The first extends from Hartland Point to Trevose Head, the coast facing westwards at the beginning and gradually swinging round, with minor dislocations on the way, to face almost north at the western end. Here we treat the part which lies between Marsland Mouth (the Devon/Cornwall border) and Port Isaac.

From Marsland Mouth as far as Rusey Beach below High Cliff the rocks are sandstones and shales of the Culm Measures of the Upper Carboniferous. Much of our knowledge of the local geology and geomorphology stems from the work of E. A. N. Arber, whose *Coastal Scenery of North Devon* (1911, recently reprinted) is essential reading for any walker on this part of the path. Of the section of high flat-topped cliffs between Hartland Point and Widemouth Sand he wrote: "It may be doubted whether any other shore line in Britain furnishes as many and as perfect examples of folded and contorted rocks as

Cliffs at Yeol Mouth

5

these." The coastline cuts at right-angles across the strata, so that magnificent cross-sections of the folds are displayed on the cliff face or as lines of reefs on the beaches. Add the great sheets of overlapping slabs and a range of stacks and beach pinnacles and we have a coast scenery of infinite variety and savage interest, one which has also attracted the climber. The contorted strata continue to Millook, then follow six or seven miles of cliff greatly modified by land-slipping. At Rusey Beach the strata change to Lower Carboniferous: black shales with some sandstones, cherts and quartz veins. After Boscastle come shales of Middle and Upper Devonian with occasional small patches of igneous outcrop.

Except for five miles in the neighbourhood of Bude all this coastline is included in the Cornwall Area of Outstanding Natural Beauty. The National Trust owns Vicarage Cliff and Hawker's Look-out at Morwenstow, part of Combe Valley, the cliffs between Combe Valley and Sandymouth, Dizzard Point, the headlands on either side of Crackington Haven, High Cliff, Boscastle Harbour and Valley, several coast properties at Tintagel (Barras Nose, Glebe Cliff and Penhallick Point), Treknow Cliff above Trebarwith, the coast between Tregonnick Tail and Jacket's Point and some sites at Port Gaverne.

Bude is the only considerable town, but even then not so formal a resort as to have a promenade. Widemouth Sand attracts many visitors, while Tintagel is a real place of pilgrimage and will always be crowded in the season. Looking out of place and therefore hard to overlook are the satellite tracking station at Cleave by Lower Sharpnose and the King Arthur's Castle Hotel at Tintagel. Nevertheless this is one of the finest sections of the path with some really magnificent and little-used stretches of cliff top. There are Youth Hostels at Boscastle and Tintagel and at Elmscott just north of Marsland Mouth in Devon.

At Hartland Point in North Devon the West Country coastline turns abruptly from the vegetation-covered north-facing cliffs of the Bristol Channel to savage rocky cliffs worn by the ceaseless beat of the Atlantic Ocean. Here the fetch is several thousand miles and the west wind builds up impressive rollers in its passage over this immense stretch of water. The line of the cliffs cuts across the strata exposing the mighty folds of the Armorican orogeny.

Some six miles to the south is the Marsland Valley, "deep with oak coppice about the upper end and with a great sweep of gorse bespangled down where the chine widens towards the sea". Close to where the narrow streamlet reaches the ocean between green hillsides buttressed by crags on the seaward side, the walker, crossing a meagre plank bridge, passes from Devon into Cornwall and to the start of the Cornwall Coast Path. The stream rises some four miles east of here within a short distance of the southbound Tamar and the easterly flowing Torridge—a notable watershed.

The small shingle beach at Marsland Mouth is the scene of dramatic events in *Westward Ho!*, in which Kingsley gives some unforgettable descriptions of the savage local scenery: "Each beach has its black field of jagged shark's-tooth rock . . . stretching in parallel lines out to the westward in strata set upright on edge, or tilted towards each other at strange angles by primeval earthquakes." Off the next headland to the south, accessible only along the shore and not readily climbable, is the first of many Gull Rocks, the one from which the legendary pirate, Cruel Coppinger, was snatched by a ghostly ship back to his netherworld. In the cove behind is the 20-metre (66 feet) fall of Litter Water, one of the most impressive cliff waterfalls in an area where there are many widely different kinds. It is, however, a sight seen better from the beach than from the path.

Ahead at Yeol Mouth a famous crag shows the typical overlapping slab structure of the shales hereabouts. The climbing is emphatically for experts. Next comes the massive Henna Cliff which rises 135 metres above the beach in a structureless conglomerate form, impressive and unclimbable. The view is wide-ranging, on one hand to Trevose Head far along the bay, with the hills of Bodmin Moor inland, on the other to Hartland Point, Lundy and the far-off hills of Wales.

Steeply down from Henna Cliff we come to the valley of Morwenstow, named, it is said, for St. Morwenna, whose well was somewhere down the face of the cliffs. There is no village, just a few scattered houses and the tiny Bush Inn. Hereabouts, a century ago, the prolix eccentric, the Rev. R. S. Hawker, had his church and vicarage, with its assorted chimney pots, miniatures of the towers of various churches and two Oxford colleges with which he had been associated. On Vicarage Cliff looking down to the cove is the "Look-out" (now National Trust) from which he scanned the seas for ships in trouble— in the days of sail in a westerly gale any ship inside the line from Trevose Head to Hartland Point was almost certainly doomed— composed poetry and elaborated his legends. Here many years later two climbers completed the first-ever climb on these cliffs which they named Hawker Slab.

Higher Sharpnose Point has a crag also and a coastguard look-out, beside which the Tidna stream produces another unusual waterfall. Stanbury Mouth, the first beach on our journey to show any quantity of sand, can be reached only on foot. Between here and Lower Sharpnose Point the cliff has suffered from continuing despoliation—once by an anti-aircraft gunnery school firing out to sea, now a satellite tracking, or early warning, station.

Now the path descends to Combe Valley, from which it is possible to walk on sand most of the way for the next three and a half miles to Bude. The official route continues on the cliff top but easy interchanges are possible. On the way we pass a diverse set of beach pinnacles: Square Block, the Flame and Ship Ashore at Sandy Mouth, the Unshore Rock at Northcott Mouth, then the Horn of Plenty and Easy Street. All along this stretch the cliffs show folds and contortions of the strata which are tilted at all angles up to the vertical; harder bands run across the beach as ribs, softer bands are sand-covered on the beaches and form clefts or chimneys between the harder strata on the cliff faces. Perhaps the best known is Maer Cliff just beyond Northcott but almost everywhere there is something to wonder at.

Bude, which has been known to call itself Britain's Bondi, has extensive sands. The large tidal range of some 16 feet leads to impressive high seas at spring tides: "The waves are mountains high, and the roar, as they break and pound the foreshore, can be heard for miles inland." Bude Canal, which formerly carried loads of sand, coal, slate and corn, is almost completely disused. Compass Point above Bude Haven, buttressed on the south by slabs of rock "set on edge like mammoth playing cards", gives tremendous views up and down the coast.

Inland, close by Stratton, is Stamford Hill, where local royalists won a famous battle in 1643. Beyond it the church at Launcells has "the best set of symbolic bench end carvings in the west". Stratton is more ancient than Bude, for, when John Leland described this coast in his report to King Henry VIII in the 1540s, he wrote: "From Stratton to Padstow the Contery by the Northe Se ys rather Hylle then Montaynenius, and ys very fertyle of Gras and Corne; and the Clives of the sayd Northe Se betwne the Places aforsayd hath good fyne blew Slates apte for Howse Kyveryng, and also hath diverse Vaynes of Leade and other metalles not yet knowen."

For two and a half miles south of Bude the path runs parallel to and never very far from the road over Efford Beacon, past a further series of beach pinnacles and slabby cliffs to the broad sands of Widemouth. Here even the crowded sands may perhaps be preferred to a route on the road or through the car parks. The prominent Black Rock, up-standing in the centre of the strand, is haunted by the ghost of the legendary wrecker Featherstone. Inland the Devon–Cornwall border, forsaking for once the Tamar, bulges to within three miles of the sea south-east of Marhamchurch. Path and road by Wanson Mouth and Penhalt Cliff lead on to the tiny cove of Millook Haven, with more contorted strata in the flanking cliffs. Penfound Manor, three miles to the east, is one of the oldest inhabited manors in the country.

Between Millook and Dizzard Point and also beyond it, the cliffs have been transformed by landslipping and in places the path is a quarter of a mile from the sea. "To walk along the edge of the landslip after dark", says Page, "would be dangerous. For the brink is full of fissures, generally running parallel with the cliff, and of uncertain depth. The worst place is a bit of common, for here the cracks are not only concealed by the gorse bushes but run in every direction." Dizzard Point is 150 metres (491 feet) high with the seaward slopes covered with trees. From Chipman Point we look down into Scrade Water, which tumbles in a fall to Cleave Strand. The next valley, Coxford Water, ends similarly. This is of particular geomorphological interest, in that the sea is simultaneously cutting back the valley mouth and eroding its north wall, so that ultimately a diversion of the stream should occur as has already happened elsewhere along the coast. The church nearby, recalling that at Morwenstow, is dedicated to St. Genesius, who, after decapitation, carried his head around.

The path climbs the south side of the valley on to Pencannow Point and descends beyond to the small beach of Crackington Haven. The far headland, Cambeak, "a gruesome place, so narrow its head, so sheer the precipice", juts out so far that it is worth a visit. The cliffs are landslipped, hummocky slopes separating the highest point, High Cliff (223 metres/729 feet), from the beaches, giving the lie to the comment that, "adventurous souls like to lie face down on its edge and gaze at the sea over 700 feet below". The beaches of the Strangles

Port Isaac

and Rusey, divided by the rocks of Voter Run, can be reached by path down the undercliff. There are beach pinnacles and an arch. At Rusey comes the change from the Upper Carboniferous to the black shales of the Lower Carboniferous, which form hog's back-type cliffs on as far as Boscastle.

A secluded section of the path leads on for two and a half miles past the dark masses of Buckator, Beeny Cliff and Fire Beacon Point into the cove of Pentargon. Offshore is the seething reef known as the Beeny Sisters. Pentargon has a cave and a waterfall. We climb over Penally Hill and descend into the Valency Valley at Boscastle.

This village grew up in the shadow of Botreaux Castle of which no trace remains. The tortuous harbour, described by Leland as "a pore Havenet of no certaine Salvegarde", is picturesque but not seriously navigable for sail through a narrow opening between black cliffs. The Cobweb Inn down by the harbour is a curiosity. Nearby is Peters Wood Nature Reserve. The headland on the south side, known as Willapark (96 metres/314 feet), is the site of a camp; between here and Forrabury Church, some third of a mile inland, is a huge open field which still shows the pattern of strip cultivation of Saxon times, or earlier.

The path continues, straightforward and easy to follow, through magnificent scenery to a second Willapark headland (93 metres/ 304 feet), also surmounted by a camp, close to Tintagel. In between we pass "the ghastly chasm" of West Blackapit, the sea stacks of Short Island, Long Island (apparently climbable as there is a cairn on 10 top, yet far from obviously so) and Lye Rock and Ladies Window

Head, named for a curious aperture in the summit rocks through which there is a fine view of the sea below. Bossiney Haven at the foot of the picturesque Rocky Valley has a sandy beach and a rock arch, known for obvious reasons as Elephant Rock. The valley, which carries a profusion of plant life with rocky outcrops here and there, runs up to and beyond the B3263 to the waterfall of St. Nectan's Kieve; it is well worth a diversion. According to legend, King Arthur's golden round table lies buried under a circular mound in an ancient earthwork at the west end of Bossiney village.

Soon we reach King Arthur's Castle Hotel on the cliff top, a landmark for many a coastal mile. Beyond is Tintagel Head with its twelfth-century castle ruins—an inner ward on the headland, the outer ward on the mainland formerly linked by a drawbridge. The two are still joined by the land-bridge, of which Carew wrote (and as some may still feel): "In many places through his stickleness occasioning and through his steepness threatening the ruin of your life with the failing of your foot." Only fragments of the castle remain, with traces of the earlier third-century Celtic religious settlement. The views from the outjutting headland are tremendous. Down below, "through it from cliffe to clyffe is a cave or vaulte, so spacious and capable as a fisher boate may pass from one syde to the other".

The village above, which is actually Trevena and not Tintagel at all, attracts large numbers of tourists drawn by the tenuous associations with King Arthur. The close ties with tourism cast an air of artificiality over something which is intrinsically scenically attractive. A service of Land-Rovers carries non-walkers down the little 11 valley from the village to the castle gate in Tintagel Cove, churning up the track and depositing it over the vegetation, imparting a scene of desolation from which the path soon escapes up the facing hill.

We climb steeply to the church of St. Materiana, prominent on its cliff top and, passing at length above a steep pinnacle left behind by quarrymen on Treknow Cliff, descend to the sands of Trebarwith Strand. Offshore is another Gull Rock, conical and 40 metres (131 feet) high.

Dennis Point (93 metres/304 feet) rises above the south end of the beach in a very steep cliff made of what looks like congealed mud. The path crosses the hill and immediately descends again into a deep valley above Blackways Cove. The next stretch is one of the quietest of the whole path. Between here and Port Gaverne, five miles ahead, there is only one ready access point—the pathway to the sands of Tregardock Beach.

Two miles inland, and well worth a visit, is Old Delabole Quarry, which has been worked for slates for close on 400 years. It is an outstanding piece of man-made landscape—a vast hole in the ground, a quarter of a mile wide and several hundred feet deep. The claim that it is "the largest single open excavation in England" depends very much on the criteria used, but it is impressive by any standards. Farther inland lies the granite block of Bodmin Moor. Brown Willy (420 metres/1,374 feet), the highest point of Cornwall, is some ten miles from the sea at Tintagel. Rough Tor close by presents a notable rocky outline with summit rocks reminiscent of Dartmoor.

The path continues over valley mouth and headland past Jacket's Point and Bounds Cliff (a mile south-east is the ancient enclosure of Tregeare Round) to the one-time fishing village of Port Gaverne. A minor road leads on to Port Isaac, a typical ancient fishing village of narrow streets with a tiny port from which Delabole slates were once shipped.

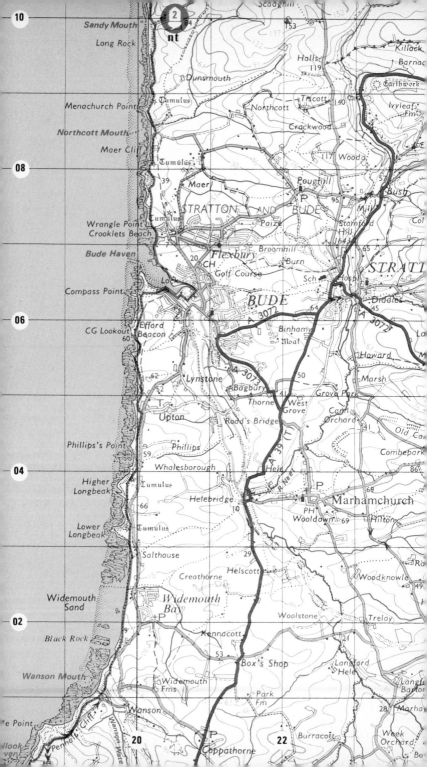

Port Isaac to Newquay

33 miles

This section includes the major ria, or drowned river valley, of the north Cornwall coast, the Camel Estuary, and ends at another only slightly less striking, that of the Gannel. Trevose Head is the outstanding point between Hartland Point and the coast of West Penwith, dividing the whole north coast into the two large bays we have already noticed. Minor indentations produce a detailed pattern in which west-facing shores gradually pass into north-facing, followed by an abrupt turn at a headland and a repetition of the process. Now there are many more beaches of sand and the big waves of these west-facing shorelines provide the incomparable surfing for which this part of Cornwall is especially noted.

These sands and the more gentle nature of the cliffs, which offer many more points of access, make this a holiday coastline dedicated to the traditional pleasures of the seaside. In this respect it provides a soft interlude between the savage rocks of the early part of the path and the mine-scarred cliffs and granite fortresses which lie ahead. Long stretches of sand are a relief after the ups and downs of the cliff path. One can walk bare-footed along the edge of the sea.

This section is all slates and shales of the Upper and Middle Devonian, with associated grits, sandstones and conglomerates. Usually the coves are worn into the softer shales, while the headlands are formed by more resistant rocks, either igneous intrusions or local material which has been metamorphosed. Thus Stepper Point, the Rumps, the islands of Gulland, Newland and the Mouls, and Park Head are all of greenstone, while Pentire Point, Porthmissen, Cataclews Point and Trevose Head are igneous. The pillow lavas of Pentire are widely known as a notable example of the latter and get their name from the curious shapes in which the rock has solidified.

The first part of this section is in the Cornwall Area of Outstanding Natural Beauty; between Bedruthan Steps and Newquay the coast was considered to be too built over to warrant designation. The National Trust owns some small sites west of Portquin, the headland of Pentire, part of Porthcothan, and holdings at either end of the strand at Bedruthan.

Newquay is a substantial resort, the largest in Cornwall, its urban area occupying around three miles of coast. Other places such as Mawgan Porth and Harlyn Bay have been developed for holiday-makers with bungalows, caravans, etc. There will be crowds almost everywhere in the season, particularly at Bedruthan Steps and on all the sandy beaches between Stepper Point and Newquay. There are no man-made follies of a more specialised and spectacular kind. The Camel has to be crossed by a ferry from Rock to Padstow. Although a regular service, the point of embarkation may vary with the state of the tide and local enquiries should be made.

Hockin voted the coastline between Port Isaac and Polzeath one of the three finest cliff sections in the whole of Cornwall, comparable with Land's End to Treryn Dinas and Gunwalloe to Kynance. But he was so repelled by the Trevose–Newquay section as to suggest striking inland by way of Wadebridge and rejoining the coast at the Gannel. There is a Youth Hostel at Treyarnon Bay.

The path climbs steeply out of Port Isaac on to Lobber Point and descends to Pine Haven. The route is planned to hug the sea's edge round Varley and Kellan Heads, but for the time being it is necessary to take a direct line across their bases to Port Quin. This is a narrow harbour on the east side of Port Quin Bay, said to have been a thriving fishing port before most of the fishermen were lost in a storm at sea. However, there seems little substance to the legend, for Norden in 1584 was already describing it as "all decayed since the growing up of Port Isaac". It seems hardly big enough anyway. The way westward has a long tradition of exclusion of the public from the coastline; Folliott-Stokes (1900s) and Hockin (1930s) both had trouble here. Now, at last, the way is straightforward with several little coves and headlands. We pass the funnel depression called Lundy Hole and come to Com Head at the beginning of the National Trust's extensive Pentire Point holding.

At this point the cliff scenery is very striking. Rumps Point, surmounted by the remains of an Iron Age camp, shows a succession of rock pinnacles on a ridge highly reminiscent of mountain scenery. There are caves below. Ahead, on Pentire Point, is a magnificent crag of pillow lava, which has only recently been climbed—by experts, it goes without saying. The Point (79 metres/257 feet) is the eastern portal of the Camel Estuary. It looks straight out over the sea for half the circle, since Stepper Point, the opposite portal, lies back somewhat, revealing Trevose Head and its lighthouse farther west. Landward are the broad waters and sand-bars of the estuary with St. Breock Downs behind.

The relative disposition of these flanking headlands probably accounts for the extensive sands, called Doom Bar, which deny river passage to all but the smallest vessels. With an easterly longshore drift, they funnel material into the estuary, from which many tons of sand are removed annually without materially improving the navigability. As Carew wrote: "The harbour is barred with banks of sand, made (through uniting their weak forces) sufficiently strong to resist the ocean's threatening billows, which find their rage subdued by the other's lowly submission." Legend has it that the bar was formed following a curse by a mermaid shot by a local man.

Exposure to the westerly fetch produces fine conditions for surfing at the tiny resorts of Pentireglaze and Polzeath. They are populated in the season, leading Betjeman to write: "Here caravans, railway carriages, shacks and bungalows have done their worst, so that one has continually to look out to sea and at National Trust property to remember Old Cornwall." We hurry on therefore past Daymer Bay, which marks this end of the Doom Bar, to St. Enodoc. There is a famous golf course and an ancient church, dating from 1400, which had to be excavated from encroaching sand. The ferry from Rock to Padstow has an ancient history, having been recorded in the fourteenth century.

Padstow, now a pleasant little resort with sands and boating, has been a port, mostly given over to fishing, for more than 1,000 years. Leland (sixteenth century) found "a good quick fisher town, but uncleanly kept" and *Murray's Guide* (nineteenth century) an "antiquated, unsavoury fishing town". Even in the 1900s Baddeley and Ward's guide-book reported that "no one deliberately visits Padstow for its own sake". All that is long past. A local curiosity is the Hobby Horse dances which take place on May Day, following some immemorial tradition. Prideaux Place is an Elizabethan manor house.

The path now returns on the west bank of the Camel by Harbour Cove, Hawkers Cove and the westerly end of the Doom Bar to Stepper Point (74 metres/242 feet). There is a 12-metre (39 feet) white daymark. The next mile of cliff between here and Gunver Head is impressively precipitous, the foot of the cliff appearing to be completely inaccessible. Only from a boat can one examine the recesses of Butter Hole, Pepper Hole and Seal Hole, though Page (1897) said that it was possible then to descend the cliff face to the first of these. It does not look possible now. At Gunver Head is the famous Tregudda Gorge, a narrow cleft between the steep main cliff and Lower Merope Island. This and the outer islands of Middle and Higher Merope have been scaled by expert climbers, but ways of doing so look far from obvious.

Next on the main cliff come the natural arches of Porthmissen Bridge, followed by the so-called Marble Cliffs, where alternate layers of slate and quartz produce an unusual walled appearance on the cliff face. On the slopes towards the sands of Trevone is the Round Hole, another funnel down to sea level. Between here and Trevose Head is a succession of fine sandy beaches, all north-facing: Trevone, Harlyn (where there is a museum of antiquities collected from a Celtic burial ground uncovered in 1900) and Mother Ivey's Bays. Cataclews Point and Merope Rocks have caves and arches. The famous Cataclews Stone is quarried nearby: blue-grey, looking like cast iron, it can be deeply carved, as shown in the fonts at Padstow and St. Merryn and the stoup at St. Endellion.

The lighthouse on Trevose Head, built in 1847, is at the approximate centre of the long northern coast of the peninsula. The headlands at the opposite ends of the bays—Hartland Point, some 40 miles away in the north-east, and the granite cliffs and hills of West Penwith, the same distance to the south-west—are visible in the clear view. At night their lights (Hartland and Lundy, Godrevy and Pendeen), even though at low levels, flash out across the broad spaces of the ocean.

Now we set off due southwards, soon passing another Round Hole on the cliff above Mackerel Cove. Separated by headlands which have survived because of their harder rocks, an almost continuous line of

sand beaches stretches between here and Newquay; all will be in busy use during the summer months. The path is invariably on the cliff top but the sands can often be crossed in suitable conditions of tide if a change of scenery is desired. We descend from Trevose Head into Booby's Bay and Constantine Bay. The ancient church of St. Constantine, just inland, is only with difficulty preserved from burial by sand. At Treyarnon Beach (Youth Hostel), Trethias Island is a Nature Reserve. An interesting line of low cliffs with caves and arches separates it from the sands of Porthcothan Beach. The green-stone Park Head follows, the start of the famous Bedruthan Steps coast—an arc of about one and a half miles between here and Carnewas Island.

The name derives from a series of rocky islets on the foreshore, said to have been used as stepping stones by the giant Bedruthan. Later the name seems to have been applied to a staircase of rock steps down the cliff face at the southern end, which was closed to the public after a rock fall which led to a fatality. Alternative lines require great care and this beach is perhaps best viewed from the safety of the cliff top. The first "Step" is Diggory's Island, where there are caves and arches; the cliff behind, with a series of tiny coves and six round barrows on the top, belongs to the National Trust. The next step is the familiar, and often photographed, Queen Bess Rock; other profiles, possibly more convincing, can be discovered around about by the highly imaginative. Now follow Samaritan Rock (where a ship of that name was wrecked), Redcove Island (with camp on the cliff above), Pendarves Island and finally the conical Carnewas Island. Two miles inland is St. Eval, an aerodrome site, its church rebuilt in the eight-eenth century as a daymark.

The path continues by the cliff edge to Mawgan Porth, a sandy beach surrounded by holiday houses. This is the mouth of the Vale of Mawgan which runs up to St. Columb Major. Beyond, some six and a half miles from the sea, is one of the major Cornish earthworks, Castle an Dinas, which crowns a granite outlier of Hensbarrow Downs, only a mile off the A30. To the north, St. Breock Downs reach 208 metres (680 feet); antiquities include the Nine Maidens, a stone avenue 350 feet long, probably having astronomical significance.

Berryl's Point, and Griffin's Point with a promontory fort, separate Mawgan Porth from the two-mile beach of Watergate Bay. This is backed by shale cliffs, in places 60 metres (196 feet) high, the path continuing to hug the edge. A low water alternative along the sands would be straightforward.

At the far end is Trevelgue Head, the beginning of Newquay. The extremity of the Head, known as Porth Island, is approached by a footbridge and carries the relics of an Iron Age camp. Between here and Towan Head (which because it juts out so far has been described as a natural pier), a series of magnificent sandy beaches faces north. There are several caverns in the cliff line—notably Banqueting Hall cave (200-feet long by 60-feet wide), Cathedral Cavern, Boulder Cavern and Fern Cavern. On the far side of Towan Head is the west-facing Fistral Beach, buttressed at the far end by Pentire Point East, the northerly portal of the Gannel.

The name Newquay has no significance, for the place was already "new" in Carew's time. For many years a fishing village, it now offers all the amenities of a well-appointed resort, including an air service. The 3-mile urban area, highly populated in the season, is unavoidable. If the path walker really wants to escape from people, he must pass this way only in the winter months; in summer he must take the opportunity of catching up with the amenities of civilisation here before setting out once again for the comparative "wilds".

The Gannel, only some ten metres (33 feet) wide at low tide, has to be crossed, preferably by ferry, otherwise by stepping stones or bridge farther upstream; local enquiries may help to locate the exact whereabouts. The relative difficulty of passing the river cuts Newquay off abruptly on this side; it is soon left behind over the hill. Inland, two-and-a-half-miles south-east, at Trerice, is a fine Elizabethan manor house.

Sea Anemone: 1 Snakelocks. 2 Beadlet. 3 Dahlia. **Seaweed:** 4 Alaria Esculenta. 5 Oarweed. 6 Bladder Wrack. 7 Saw Wrack. **Shells:** 8 Variegated Scallop. 9 Tower Shell. 10 Dog Whelk. 11 Common Limpet. 12 Purple Topshell. 13 Edible Crab

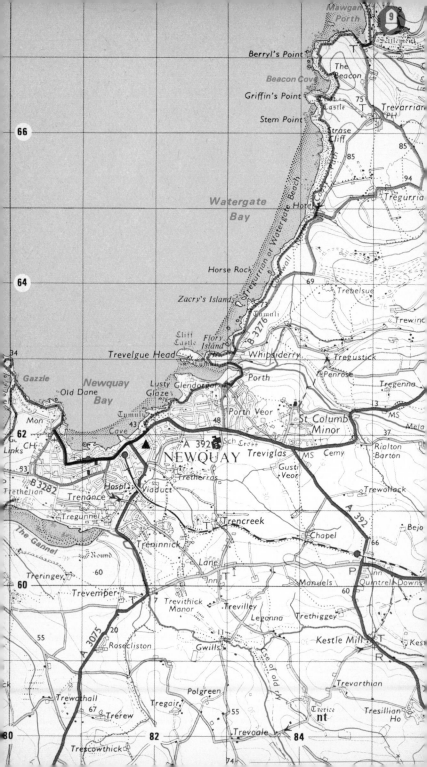

Newquay to St. Ives

39 miles

The westbound walker meets a variety of new scenes in this stretch of coastline: two extensive areas of blown sand at Penhale Sands in Perran Bay and the Towans in St. Ives Bay, and the first considerable relics of the ancient mining industry. At St. Ives, with the mountain-like hills of West Penwith looming excitingly ahead, we reach the end of the second of the large north-coast bays. Beyond is the "toe" of the peninsula, a solid block of mainly granite country which is the end of the land.

The slates and shales of the Upper and Middle Devonian continue, except that Cligga Head by Perranporth and the Beacon, just inland at St. Agnes, are granite outliers. Since it was the intrusion of the granite into the present surface rocks which metamorphosed them and concentrated the metalliferous ore-bearing veins, it is not surprising to find the relics of mining activity scattered over a wide area. Ore specimens and even mineral single crystals may reward the diligent searcher on cliffs, beaches or spoil heaps. Many travellers have noted the variegated colouring of the cliff faces—"streaked with pink and white and dove greys", "rich buffs and browns", and so on.

Farther on between Portreath and Godrevy, the fine cliffs of Reskajeage Downs are the abrupt edge of a flat plateau area, a former raised beach which looks as though it had been sliced off with a knife. Inland around the northern edge of the Carnmenellis granite massif is the huge mining complex of Redruth and Camborne, the largest and ugliest in the county.

There are three latter-day obstructions in this section and they will be with us for a long time to come. Between Holywell Bay and Ligger Point at the northern end of Penhale Sands is an area of coastline in use as an Army range or training ground and closed to the public. Even though it is said to be little used for training and can be walked over when warning flags are not flying, the official path skirts it by a detour inland. Negotiations are taking place for access to this area but meantime local enquiries should be made. Between Porthtowan and Portreath is the Government Defence Establishment of Nancekuke. The path continues outside the perimeter fence along the cliff edge, but it is closed off at certain times when potentially dangerous processes are in train. Miscellaneous industrial development at Hayle, unavoidable until there is a ferry once again across the Hayle River, adds nothing to the environment.

It is necessary to have a point of view about the relics of tin and 29 copper mining, which, of course, have no pretensions to beauty in any shape or form. They involved the complete destruction of the natural landscape and deserved much the same condemnation as we reserve for our own present-day activities in environmental despoliation. However, as we cannot remove them and as nature is working valiantly to topple and overgrow them, we have to accept the characteristic chimney stacks, engine houses and so on as an inescapable part of the landscape. These progressively deteriorating ruins add variety to the enjoyment of a walk which in their active days they would have largely nullified. At the time, of course, they were symbols of a prosperity for which the destruction of the cliff scenery was just a part of the price to be paid, and visitors came to see the mines in operation without caring much one way or the other about their effect on the natural surroundings.

The Cornwall Area of Outstanding Natural Beauty includes all the cliff line from Perranporth to Godrevy Towans, except for the Nancekuke section. The National Trust owns some small properties round the Gannel, Kelsey Head, Holywell Beach, a small islet known as the Chick, St. Agnes Beacon, Wheal Coates Mine, Chapel Porth Beach and valley, and finally six continuous miles of cliff over Carvannel, Reskajeage and Hudder Downs between Portreath and Godrevy Towans.

Two ferries are involved in the best possible route, but neither is particularly vital as the alternatives are convenient anyway. As mentioned on page 24, the Gannel is crossed by ferry, on the outskirts of Newquay, probably plying only in daylight hours in the holiday season. The ferry across the Hayle River does not operate at present though there is hope that it will be restored. The detour by road is only three miles, but passes unfortunately through industrial Hayle and along short stretches of the A30 and A3074. The ferry would enable the steadfast walker to turn his back on all this.

Perranporth and St. Ives are busy small resorts crowded in summer months, but their influence does not spread far up or down the coast. There is a Youth Hostel at Phillack by Hayle.

It was Folliott-Stokes who suggested 60 years ago that a dam on the Gannel would turn it into a pleasant lake for visitors to Newquay; this fate is still happily withheld. In fact the river is a moat staying any southward spread. Ferry or stepping stones bring the traveller to the far shore, which at low tide may just be the extensive sands that reach on to Crantock Beach. Beyond is Pentire Point West, followed by Kelsey Head (with a two-and-a-half-acre promontory fort) and the islet called the Chick offshore. Now comes Holywell Beach with blown sand inland and two fantastic beach pinnacles, one at either end. The eponymous holy well is on the north side.

Ahead over Penhale and Ligger Points is the military range, and the path turns inland by way of Ellenglaze, Trebisken, Mount and Gear, before returning to the sea's edge via the famous church of St. Piran. "The oldest Christian building in Cornwall, perhaps in Britain," it dates from the sixth or seventh century and has been buried by drifting sands, periodically lost and found throughout its history. There is now a protective concrete outer cover and a large white cross marks the site. Nearby is a two-and-a-half-metre granite monolith called Perran Cross. The dunes hereabouts reach well over 60 metres (200 feet) in places. Beneath these sands lies the buried city of Langarrow, said to have stretched from the Gannel to Perranporth. After turning into a West Country Sodom, it was overwhelmed by storm and sand. Eventually the sand hills give way to low dark cliffs with caves and mine workings and we come to Perranporth, a small holiday resort, highly populated in the season, with no promenade. Inland (1¼ miles) is the ancient amphitheatre of St. Piran Round.

Over Droskyn Point, where there are mine adits on the cliff face, we come to Cligga Head and the first granite. This was once the site of a dynamite works belonging to Nobel of the Peace Prize. At the turn of the century the scene was described as: "Tall chimneys, large buildings and insulating sheds of this great manufactory of high explosives . . . suspicious looking boilers and evil looking tanks . . . sinister little black sheds with red roofs surrounded by earthworks . . . a terrible eyesore, placed as it is so conspicuously on the summit of the cliff." Only scanty relics remain though the scars on the land will take a long time to heal. Three separate ruins of mining enterprises and the presence of modern equipment heralding a possible revival add up to a scene of devastation from which we hasten to escape.

St. Agnes is about two miles ahead. The cliffs between, reaching to 90 metres (300 feet) and more, and the valleys of Trevellas and Trevaunance, which here come down to the sea, are strewn with mine workings. At Trevellas the cliff faces are notably coloured. Trevaunance Cove, now a bathing beach with the usual amenities, was once a port from which copper and tin ore were shipped; vessels came in at the cliff foot and were loaded from staging up above. Again Folliott-Stokes comments on the industrial scene as he found it: "On the beach itself a great overshot wheel revolves, and discharges dirty water on to the already discoloured sand. On the hill-side above are more wheels, slowly-moving chains, mud heaps, and smoking chimneys; while the loud and ceaseless chatter of stamps fills the air with noise. . . . The sides of the cliffs are scarred with adits, and the surrounding water, instead of aquamarine, is the colour of pea soup."

St. Agnes Beacon (192 metres/628 feet) rises above the town. It is a worthwhile viewpoint: up and down the north coast from Trevose Head to Clodgy Point beyond St. Ives, across to the south coast with Falmouth Harbour and St. Michael's Mount prominent, and to the hills of West Penwith, Carnmenellis, Hensbarrow Downs and Bodmin Moor. The landscape in every direction is studded with mine chimneys, but are they solely relics of the past? Over all broods the threat that the search for tin may be pursued once again, and with the same callous indifference to the countryside.

The cliff top path continues past more mine ruins towards St. Agnes Head. Below the cliff hereabouts is the Seal Hole Cavern, which in 1823 was the scene of a large tea party with singing and dancing. It could be entered either from the beach or by the shaft of North Seal Hole Mine. A mile offshore are the reefs variously known as Bowden Rocks, Man and His Man or Cow and Calf, which identify this point in many a distant view. The Head is a minor turning point in the coastline which here changes from east-west to north-south. The path continues southwards past more mines (including Wheal 31

St. Agnes Head

Coates which is being restored by the National Trust), though not as many as before. So we reach the beach of Chapel Porth (more caves) and a stretch of sand which leads on at low tide to Porth Towan. The path, of course, continues at the cliff top.

On the sands past Porth Towan is a beach islet, the Tobban Horse. The path above soon comes up against the barbed-wire fences of Nancekuke; we are confined to a narrow swathe between the perimeter fence and the cliff edge. At both ends, fences run from the perimeter down to the sea with gates which may sometimes be found shut if there is likely to be any danger to walkers on the cliffs. At such times the detour on the inland side is considerable. The fence and the awe-inspiring distant buildings are inescapable and reinforce, perhaps, the feeling that, even allowing for Cligga Head and Trevellas and Trevaunance Coves, we despoil a landscape much more effectively than any of our predecessors. On the last headland before Portreath Harbour is a small daymark, which serves walkers as well as mariners. Close inland are two interesting museum sites—at Mawla an unusual and highly interesting collection of farm implements and, between Portreath and Redruth, an active works, the Tolgus Tin Company, engaged in tin streaming.

Portreath is now mostly resort, though the small harbour is still operational. Now follows the fine cliff line over Carvannel, Reskajeage and Hudder Downs, of which we have already spoken. It is

straightforward, open going along a substantially flat cliff top, though the proximity of the B3301 makes this a popular picnic spot for motorists. The cliff faces are steep, though seldom enough to please the practised rock climber. The rock scenery is striking at the curiously named Ralph's Cupboard, as it is again at Hell's Mouth, where there is a car park close by on the road and many tourists are attracted to peer over the edge into the depths of the cove. There is a fragment of a camp on the cliff behind Samphire Island.

Inland the ground level falls away towards the conurbation of Camborne and Redruth. It is sufficiently far away not to intrude on the enjoyment from the path of the cliffs and the sea. However, the walker may diverge to see the beam engines and the engine houses of East Pool and Agar Mines, beautifully restored by the National Trust. He may visit the interesting museum at Holman's (mainly machinery, photographs and a beam engine) and at the Royal School of Mines (rocks, minerals and crystals) at Camborne. He may climb Carn Brea (225 metres/736 feet), a bastion of the Carnmenellis moors, which, surmounted by an ancient camp and a monument to Lord de Dunstanville, gives a bird's eye view of the devastation below, as well as the coastlines near and far.

From the "gruesome view" down into Hell's Mouth, the road cuts across the base of the peninsula to a bridge over the Red River, and the path reaches the same point by way of the cliff edge round Navax 33 and Godrevy Points. Offshore on an island is the unmanned Godrevy lighthouse (1859), the first since Trevose Head. The next at Pendeen is only 13 miles farther on, since the important marine crossroads at Land's End warrants the more frequent signposting. Nevertheless Pendeen is not in direct view here as it is obscured by the hills of West Penwith.

We cross the Red River, which got its name from the coloured mining spoil coming down from Camborne, and enter on the lengthy and dismal dune area of Upton Towans, backed by bungalows, chalets and caravan parks. Nearby is Gwithian, where the ancient oratory of St. Gothian has been reburied in sand and lost. The dunes lead on towards Hayle with views across to the busy west coast of the bay.

Eighty years ago *Black's Guide* said of Hayle: "A dirtier, squalider, less interesting town is not to be found in all Cornwall." Even today there is not much cause to linger, especially when our route takes us along the A30 and A3074. Some day, maybe, there will once again be a ferry from the Towans across to Porth Kidney Sands, which the path now follows in close proximity to the railway. We come by way of the urban area of Carbis Bay (more fine sands) into St. Ives.

It is more than a century since *Murray's Guide* found St. Ives "abominably tainted with the effluvia of fish cellars". Later it became famous as an artists' colony and began to grow as a resort. Narrow streets and a constricted site should continue to hinder over-development. The promontory known as the Island serves as a pier separating the east-facing harbour and Porthminster Beach from the north-facing Porthmeor Beach. Shelter from the prevailing westerlies is well contrived and utilised. The Island carried one of the first lighthouses, a chapel of St. Nicholas, which in Leland's day was "a pharos for lighte for shippes sailing by night".

Inland the West Penwith hills begin at Trencrom, Trink Hill and Rosewall Hill. The first, which is National Trust property, carries an Iron Age hill fort with a single wall. There is a wide view over the seas north and south and up-country to Trevose Head and Brown Willy. To the south-east the neck of land between St. Erth and Marazion is so low that West Penwith only just escapes being an island.

Note for Map 10
Pending negotiations to allow access to the approved coastal path, at present inaccessible because of the Ministry of Defence firing range, the alternative inland route should be followed.

St. Ives to Penzance

34 miles

The fifth of the line of granite bosses, which are strung from end to end of the West Country, forms a substantial part of West Penwith beyond the line St. Erth–Marazion. There are slates and shales of the Devonian also, known locally as killas, and volcanic rocks—greenstone—of the same period. The interaction between these rocks and granite, which welled up in a molten state during the Carboniferous period, led to the formation of the metalliferous ore deposits characteristic of the north and west coasts of the peninsula. As Carew wrote: "The cliffs thereabouts muster long streaks of glittering hue, which import a show of copper; and copper mines are found and wrought in the grounds adjoining." Later, tin was found by going deeper in the same mines. Greenstone and killas outcrop between St. Ives and Porthmeor and between Pendeen and Cape Cornwall. Granite fills in between these on the north coast and continues from Cape Cornwall round Land's End and back along the south coast as far as Lamorna; then it is greenstone and killas to Penzance.

The granite is exposed in a form which is highly characteristic. Because of prominent horizontal and vertical jointing the cliffs appear from afar to rise in square-cut towers and walls as though constructed from giant masonry. The word "Cyclopean" is often applied. The rock, which crystallised out slowly beneath the earth's surface and has been exposed subsequently by denudation, exhibits a surface covered with large crystals among which the constituent minerals, quartz, felspar and mica, can be readily detected. In sheltered places a luxuriant coating of lichen, from sage green through to orange, entirely hides these crystals, forcing the rock climber to burrow in search of his holds. The inland hills, reaching to around 300 metres (1,000 feet), have an air of real mountains many times as high, particularly where the higher summits look down on the sea on the northern rim. These moorland hills are a land of their own, entirely remote from and no longer within sound of the sea. Andrews has written: "It seems as if distant sounds were blanketed by an invisible barrier on these uplands where you seldom hear the sea. . . . There is a stillness which is unique."

This is a prolific site for antiquities, comparable with certain of the chalk downland ridges of Wessex. There are hill-top and promontory forts of the Iron Age, village sites, standing stones and circles and burial sites, many worthy of a diversion by the coastwise walker.

Nowadays the West Country is a major rock climbing area in its own right. The sport began here in West Penwith (see page 110) and from being the somewhat esoteric pleasure of the few for half a century, suddenly blossomed into quite fierce activity. The granite lends itself to climbing since the prominent horizontal and vertical joints convert to ledges, cracks and chimneys, while the general roughness of the surface, studded with big crystals, produces ideal foot- and hand-holds.

The official path ends at Penlee Point beyond Mousehole and there is no designated route through the urban areas of Newlyn and Penzance. This is the only substantial town, while the path often misses smaller places altogether. There are no monstrosities of the modern age by the way and no ferries to modify the planning. Except for Penzance–Newlyn all the cliff and much of the moor is Cornwall Area of Outstanding Natural Beauty, while in National Trust keeping are: Hor Point, Tregerthen Cliff, Zennor Head, Rosemergy and Trevean Cliffs along the north coast, a fine example of a beam engine at the Levant Mine near Pendeen, Mayon and Trevescan Cliffs at Sennen, and a tremendous cliff property stretching from Nanjizal to St. Levan, Treen Cliff, Pedn Vounder and Treryn Dinas, followed by Cribba Head and Penberth Cove.

The going varies considerably along the coast. That on the north coast from St. Ives to Pendeen, even though on the line of the old coastguard path, used to be particularly rough and difficult to follow, so that the field path, parallel but some distance inland, used often to be recommended as an alternative. Considerable improvements have been made in recent years which increasing traffic should do much to maintain. On the other hand, the path from Land's End to Porthgwarra has always been straightforward and free of vegetation, so that the walker is free to enjoy the scenery of what is generally regarded as the finest stretch of cliff in the West Country. From Penberth to Mousehole is another secluded coastline, where access used to be difficult; the path may help but not, it is hoped, to bring about too great a swing the other way.

West Penwith is perhaps the most foreign part of Cornwall, the most Celtic, and the most akin to Brittany. The mines of the St. Just area have devastated the countryside but we now accept the ruins as part of the natural landscape, which contribute to its essential quality. As the price of metals continues to rise there is some danger that mining may become economic once again, so the eventual despoliation could be even greater. There is, however, little likelihood of other change. The cliffs are high, the coves small and often difficult to reach, road access to the edge of the sea or the cliffs is infrequent, and many car parks are inadequate from sheer lack of space. Extensive holiday exploitation beyond the present is therefore unlikely. Many miles of cliff top should remain walkers' territory for a long time to come. There are Youth Hostels at St. Just and Penzance.

Leaving Porthmeor Beach at St. Ives, the path climbs to Clodgy Point and continues westwards on greenstone cliffs. The reef known as the Carracks is said to be a haunt of seals. At Wicca Pool an intrusion of granite takes the form of a 20-metre (65-foot) rock pillar, Wicca

Cape Cornwall—looking NE

Pinnacle. This is quiet and secluded country, remote from the coast road. Next comes Zennor Head flanked by the tiny sand coves of Porthzennor and Pendour. Inland is the hamlet of Zennor, where the granite church has unique carvings of mermaids on the ends of the pews. On Zennor Hill is the famous Zennor Quoit, surrounded by outcroppings of natural granite of typically grotesque shapes.

We continue above Porthglaze Cove to the outjutting Gurnard's Head—"the figure of a Sphinx, the entire body lying out from the cliff". There is an Iron Age promontory fort with a series of banks and ditches defending the neck. Inland beyond the hamlet of Porthmeor are more antiquarian remains: the cromlech of Mulfra Quoit, hut circles alongside the Penzance road, and two ancient village sites at Porthmeor and Bosporthennis. The first big outcrop of granite is in Porthmeor Cove.

Now the inland hills reach a magnificence of proportion and appearance—real mountains in spite of their diminutive height; the impression is heightened by exposures of bare rock and extensive boulder fields arduous to negotiate. The ridge has come from above St. Ives by way of Rosewall, Trendrine and Zennor Hills and offers the westbound walker a very good alternative route. The notably rocky hills here are Hannibal's Carn and Carn Galver; the highest point of the ridge is Watchcroft (252 metres/824 feet), half a mile ahead. To the south the lonely chimney of Ding Dong Mine rises on the desolate moorlands of the dip slope.

At Bosigran Head, surmounted by the relics of an ancient camp, the granite culminates in really stupendous cliffs dropping into Porthmoina Cove. This face, the rocky promontory of Porthmoina Island jutting out into the cove below, and the pinnacled ridge on the far side provide some of the best rock climbing. The scene here is completed by the chimney of Carn Galver Mine and the rock-strewn slopes leading up to Carn Galver. At one time a white patch painted on the face was used by the keepers of Pendeen Light to gauge the visibility, so they knew when to sound the foghorn.

The flat shelf between the cliff top and the inland hills, very marked at this point, indicates a beach of a former coastline now high above sea level. The St. Ives–St. Just road runs along this shelf, never very close to the cliff edge, sometimes as much as a mile inland; there are thus few points of access by road to the path or the sea.

Impressive granite cliffs continue to excite the eye. Up ahead the white column of the lighthouse at Pendeen looms on the skyline promontory. On the inland moors behind Watchcroft are Lanyon Quoit (the remains of a chambered long barrow, restored in 1824), a stone circle called the Nine Maidens and the curious holed stone of Men an Tol (creep through and you will never be the same again!). Below the cliffs, Zawn Alley Island is much favoured by the Great Black-backed Gull.

The path passes to the seaward of the hamlet of Morvah, above which the inland hills are again rich in antiquities: the tremendous Iron Age hill fort of Chûn Castle (two ramparts and ditches with a diameter of 280 feet overall) and, nearby, the cromlech, Chûn Quoit. Portheras Cove has a sandy beach accessible only by trackway. Beyond the Cove is Pendeen Watch lighthouse, constructed in 1900. Here the granite ends and the slate begins. A few hundred yards inland is the well-preserved fogou of Pendeen Vau.

We have now reached a stretch of coast once given over almost entirely to mining, at first copper, then tin, arsenic, and tungsten. Indeed one of the mines, Geevor, in the next cove beyond the lighthouse, functions still. Once again industrial archaeology and the works of man have to supersede our appreciation of the wonders of nature. Crystal and mineral hunting in spoil heaps and on beaches and cliff faces, attempts to re-create the past from the clues of the present, become the orders of the day. But we have to keep a wary eye open for the occasional unprotected shaft or tottering wall.

Soon comes the famous Levant Mine, whose workings ran out for a mile under the sea to a depth of 600 metres (2,000 feet). The National Trust now preserves a Cornish beam engine here. The past is re-created for us by Folliott-Stokes, for this is what he found: "Descending the valley, we climb the opposite hill, past mud and miners, arsenic fumes and tramlines, till we reach the top. But the face of the land is still marred and rendered hideous by mining operations. The path winds bravely westwards, but no longer through flowers and ferns, but over a stunted and blasted heath, or common, almost denuded of vegetation, and punctuated with little dynamite store sheds whose lightning conductors clatter in the breeze, and unsightly refuse heaps of rock and clay."

A mile farther on is Botallack Head where the ruined engine houses are perched on ledges on the cliffs. At the turn of the century visitors paid 10s. a head to descend the mine. They included Queen Victoria and Prince Albert and later the Prince and Princess of Wales, the Princes alone making the descent on each occasion. Inland is the mining hamlet of Botallack with the rocky tor of Carn Kenidjack on the hills behind. The coast is now running almost north and south; the next headland, Cape Cornwall, almost as far west as Land's End, is reached by way of the promontory fort of Kenidjack Castle. Offshore are the reefs of the Brisons.

Cape Cornwall, the only cape in England, carries a prominent mine chimney, which must surely serve as a daymark. St. Just, a tiny former mining town, is close by inland; the ancient amphitheatre of Plane an Gwarry is worth a diversion. The path passes an interesting barrow on Carn Gloose, then crosses Porth Nanven to Progo where there is a fine arch on the sands. After Aire Point the sands of Whitesand Bay can be followed, the tide permitting, as far as Sennen Cove. The path continues on the edge of gently sloping cliffs to arrive at the same place.

The inland hills end one and a half miles to the east at Carn Brea (200 metres/654 feet), which with its impressive view over the encircling seas and coasts might well be called the last hill in England. Still farther east between Bartinney Down and Caer Bran is the well-preserved fogou of Carn Euny; other antiquarian remains in the same vicinity include the 75-foot-diameter stone circle of Boscowen-un. While all these hill features have been dealt with piecemeal here as successive divergences from the coast route, they could, of course, all be connected by a continuous hill walk running parallel to the coast, as indicated above.

Sennen Cove is sheltered from the west and south-west by the headland of Pedn Mên Du, which throws down an impressive climbers'

crag on the seaward side, well seen as we continue on our way. A delightful and very popular route on open cliff top leads by way of Maen Castle fort for three-quarters of a mile to Land's End. Long-ships lighthouse marks a line of reefs offshore. Dr. Syntax's Head, below the "First and Last House", is the most westerly point and thus the true "End". Dr. Johnson's Head, below the hotel and car park at the end of the A30, suffices for the majority of visitors, and indeed is somewhat more impressive.

This is certainly the most popular place of pilgrimage in the whole of Cornwall; here thousands come every summer, every day of summer, to gaze out westwards towards America. Car parks, a hotel, cafés and curio shops cater for their needs. Yet this bristly wall of castellated granite is a fitting climax to the narrowing promontory of the county. The walker who shuns company and who has found his solitude on the coast to the north, and will recapture it again half a mile to the south, must accept his fellow-man at this point, consoling himself perhaps that such concentrations help to keep other places comparatively free. A study from time to time of the human race and its reactions to circumstances will widen the experience even of one whose first love is isolation amid natural scenery. Otherwise come of a morning or evening, or in winter time.

We turn then the corner of western England and follow the path south-eastwards past the islands of Enys Dodnan and Armed Knight. The cliff line from here to Porthgwarra is the finest in the West Country and indeed, say Baddeley and Ward, "as fine as any in these islands". After half a mile, and completely isolated from the crowds at Land's End, comes Pordenack Point where the granite cliff scenery is appreciably finer. There are two wonderful Alpine-type ridges, one all pinnacles like the fingers of a hand, the other carrying a prominent perched block—the Helmet.

The path crosses open cliff tops with no more than diminutive vegetation, passing a striking succession of headlands: Carn Boel, Carn Lês Boel (with an outjutting wall-like promontory) and Carn Barra, separated by the pleasant coves of Mill Bay (Nanjizal) and Pendower, and comes finally to Tol-Pedn-Penwith—the "holed headland."

This is the most southerly point on this side of Mount's Bay and is perhaps the culminating example of granite cliff scenery, "rising sheer as though built by Titans". Five great buttresses, falling steeply to the sea and surmounted by a coastguard look-out, are much used by climbers. Nearby are two giant markers aligned on the Runnel Stone Reef a mile out to sea, where a whistling buoy can be heard moaning whenever the wind is blowing. Much farther out is Wolf Rock lighthouse. There are good viewpoints on either side of the crags, but particularly on the eastern where easy slopes lead down past the great funnel hole (from which the head gets its name) almost to sea level.

The path continues to the tiny village of Porthgwarra; there are tunnels in the low cliffs beside the beach. The cliffs are gentler now and we soon pass St. Levan Church and the picturesque Minack

Botallack Mine as it looked in its active days

Theatre high on the cliff face, where open-air productions are staged during summer months, to reach the shell-sand beach of Porthcurno. It tends to be overcrowded, which takes away some of the delight. There are legends of a ghostly fully rigged ship which drives straight onshore to disappear up the valley.

Half a mile ahead is the National Trust holding of Treryn Dinas; one can cover the distance along the sands at low tide, the path continuing at the cliff edge. This is a rocky promontory with a series of Iron Age defensive works across the neck. There is a chaos of granite boulders including what is perhaps the most famous of the logan (rocking) stones. This one was overturned by an irresponsible Naval party during the last century and had to be replaced at the personal expense of the officer-in-charge. This point too is much visited by tourists who leave their cars in a large park in Treen village. But ahead on the coastline the story is different.

The next three or four miles are as secluded as any in the West Country. As we proceed the cliff scenery becomes ever gentler and the vegetation more lush. The local micro-climate is said to be excellent, St. Loy being one of the warmest places in the British Isles. Tater Du, which is greenstone, has an unmanned lighthouse of recent vintage and a climbers' crag. A mile inland, a stone circle, the Merry Maidens, and standing stones called The Pipers lie close to the B3315. The granite ends finally at Lamorna Cove, another site made famous by artists.

The path traces out the cliff edge all round to Mousehole, one-time fishing village, now a small resort, breaks off for its urban area, then continues beyond to Penlee Point. Now comes a break of some three and a half miles through the contiguous towns of Newlyn and Penzance. There are vast active quarries at Penlee. Newlyn is a thriving fishing port. Penzance, the urban centre of West Penwith, has a fine museum, some excellent libraries, and tropical plants thrive in the public gardens.

Botallack Head
The Crowns
16
Zawn a Bal
Wheal Edward Zawn
Nineveh
Mine (dis)
135
Wheal Bal B
Hill MS
3318
Woon
Co
Carnyorth
203
Carnyorth Circle
Carn Kenidjack
Bosloy
Botallack
PH
Kenidjack Castle
Chy
Chy
Kenidjack
130
Stone Circle
Tumuli
Porth Ledden
Boscean
Chy
Chy
Tregeseal
32
CG Lookout
Cape Cornwall
Chapel
80
90
Bostraze
Busvargus
Wks
Priest's Cove
CG Station
110
Sch
90
T
ST JUST
3071
Chy
191
Chy
Carn Gloose
94
Chy
New Downs
MS
WT Sta
MS
Wks
Chambered Cairn
The ons
Porth Nanven
Bosorne
Carrallack
Cemy
148
Crookhorn
Leswi
Nanven
Carn Leskys
Bosavern
Chy
Progo
101
Bosworlas
95
Dowran
177
Gribba Point
Little Hendra
Kelynack
30
Polpry Cove
Hendra
Maen Dower
Trevegean
116
Numphra
134
Bartinney Down
224
Gazick
Nanquidno
119
Joppa
Settlement
87
81
Land's End (St Just) Aerodrome
Carn Grean
Tredinney
Gurland
Carn Aire
127
Tumulus
Aire Point
Tregiffian
Brea
Carn Brea
200
28
Tumulus
NT
Crows
Whitesand Bay
Tumulus
Trevedra
120
MS
Treave
Cairn
MS
114
Carn Barges
Escalls
Cowloe
Sunny Corner
Trevorian
Rissick
The Tribbens
LB Sta
CG Lookout
Pedn-mên-du
Inn
Hotel
Sennen Cove
MS
T
99
Treveal
94
Röspann
26
Irish Lady
79
P
86
73
Bosanketh
Gamper
Mayon Cliff
Mayon
Dr Syntax's Head
NT
101
Cemy
Penrose
PH
Sennen
Brew
se Pea
END
Hotel
71
A 30
WT Sta
Bosfranken
Well
's Head
Carn Kez
66
T
85
Trevescan
Skewjack Fm
Trengothal
Crean
might
Corn Greeb
73
68
Enys Dodnan
Trevilley
B 3315
Trebehor
Sp.
34
Point
67
36
91
38
ottoms
24
Zawn Reeth

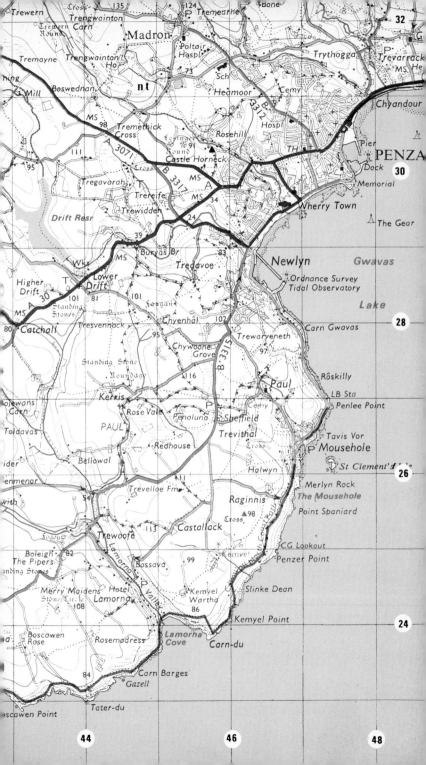

Penzance to Helford River

44 miles

After the first ten miles the granite, which has been with us for some length of time now, is at last left behind. Here we round the most southerly point of the county, and indeed of the mainland of England. A new series of igneous and metamorphosed rocks is encountered, providing the characteristic scenery of the Lizard Peninsula—hornblende schist, serpentine, gabbro and a variety of granite different from that of the rest of the county.

Along the western coast of the Lizard the serpentine makes a poor subsoil and the cliff tops are moorland with only scanty vegetation; the cliff faces, however, are steep and varied. On the east side on the other hand there is a richer soil, the cliffs are gentler and the valleys filled with vegetation. The Helford River which cuts off the Lizard Peninsula from the populous area of Falmouth is another ria. The whole peninsula escapes being entirely cut off by water only by virtue of a gap of half a mile between the head-waters of the Helford River and the Cober which runs through Helston to The Loe.

The Loe, the largest natural lake in the county, is cut off from the sea by a shingle bank very similar to, though much smaller than, the other famous bars of the West Country: Chesil Beach, Slapton Sands, the Popple at Westward Ho!, and so on. The process of its formation is not entirely understood; longshore drift will produce a bar growing down-current, but the emerging river usually maintains a breach. The final closure must have been caused by some large-scale short-term phenomenon, such as a tidal wave. Legend blames it on the giant Tregagle, universal scapegoat for this sort of occurrence all over the county.

St. Michael's Mount, Rinsey and Trewavas Heads are granite, otherwise it is killas (slates and shales of the Devonian period) as far as Gunwalloe. Schists then take over to Mullion and serpentine onwards to Kynance Cove, except for Predannack Head which is schistose. Schists all round the tip of the peninsula give way to serpentine again from Church Cove at Landewednack, on as far as Coverack. There are odd outcrops of gabbro and granite here and there, a substantial exposure of the former is quarried at Porthoustock. Finally the section is completed by a further complex area of slates and shales.

Once we leave behind the last of the granite at Trewavas Head there are no further relics of mining. Stone is quarried in some places in the peninsula: extensively for road metal at Porthoustock, where

the continuing large attacks on the gabbro enforce a detour inland for the path; on a small scale for distinctively marked varieties of serpentine, which is the basis of a local industry producing carved ornaments; on a smaller scale still for steatite (soapstone). The satellite tracking radar "dish" aerials loom inland on Goonhilly Downs, but are far enough away not to obtrude seriously on the coast walker.

There are no major coastal towns between Penzance and Falmouth, just villages and coves. Nevertheless two locations attract large numbers of tourists: Lizard Town at the end of the road and centre of the serpentine carving industry, and the famous Kynance Cove, probably the best known cove in Cornwall. Here an experiment is under way to combat erosion resulting from over-use, including resurfacing, realignment and signposting of paths. Explanatory material is available for visitors.

The only ferry is that which transports us across the Helford River at the end of the section. The value of the one-time ferry across Gillan Harbour is minimal; wading is practical at low tide and the detour by road is short anyway.

St. Michael's Mount

The Cornwall Area of Outstanding Natural Beauty starts at St. Michael's Mount and includes the whole coastline as far as Falmouth (except for a short length in the environs of Porthleven), as well as much of the interior of the Lizard Peninsula. The National Trust holds St. Michael's Mount, Lesceave Cliff at the end of Praa Sands, the cliffs between Church and Poldhu Coves, the Marconi Memorial by Poldhu Point, sites at Polurrian, Mullion Cove and Island, Predannack Head and others thereabouts. Also in National Trust hands are Kynance Cove, Lizard Downs, Bass Point, the cliffs by the Devil's Frying-pan at Cadgwith, Beagle Point by Black Head, Lowland Point by Coverack, and properties round the Helford River.

Every traveller passing through Penzance should make a point of visiting the Isles of Scilly, reached by boat in some two and a quarter hours or half an hour by helicopter (more expensive and less romantic). These islands, the fragmentary remains of the most westerly of the granite intrusions, have a charm and personality all their own. Walks along the cliff tops of the larger islands are comparable with those of the mainland path, yet infinitely more varied. The walker must necessarily have travelled in all directions by the time he returns to his starting point. Gazing out over the many other islands, one takes in the astonishing variety of scene, changing shape and form with the rise and fall of the tide.

Leaving behind the amenities of Penzance we set out eastwards from close to the railway station; the path soon runs along the edge of the sands. "When Lizard is clear, rain is near", says the local weather lore, so that the walker can estimate his chances of a fine day right at the outset by looking out across the Bay. The beach from here to Marazion past Chyandour and Long Rock has a reputation as a source of varied polished pebbles and some semi-precious stones, such as agate and chalcedony. Nowadays it is probably necessary to find more obscure beaches for any reasonable reward from this rather exciting pursuit.

St. Michael's Mount, which towers over the Bay, has a modernised castle standing on a conical hill of granite, connected to the mainland by a causeway at low water. There is a small and ancient harbour. Before the castle was built, there was a Benedictine priory, an appanage of the similar though larger-scale Mont St. Michel in Normandy.

Just over two miles inland on the southern slope of the moorland hills are the notable antiquities of Chysauster, an ancient village with houses and site carefully preserved. The Iron Age fort of Castle an Dinas—three lines of ramparts diameter 750 feet—caps a hill (233 metres/762 feet). The land is only some five miles wide at this point, so the accessibility to the northern coast path of these places of interest can be readily gauged.

The cliffs ahead are low and of easy slope with some big beaches at Perran Sands and Praa Sands. By the outjutting Cudden Point, which has a splendid view up and down the coast, are the three small coves: Prussia, Bessy's and Piskies, which were notorious smugglers' retreats in days gone by. Beyond are Praa Sands, with slight ruins of a sixteenth-century castle at Pengersick, followed by the last great granite headlands, Rinsey and Trewavas Heads. The mine workings

Kynance Cove

on the cliff edge recall those at Botallack; here too the tunnels went out beneath the sea. Two miles to the north, Tregonning Hill (194 metres/634 feet) gives wide views all over the Bay; there are anti-quarian relics also. A mile farther north-west is Godolphin Hill (162 metres/530 feet) which belongs to the National Trust. Next on the coast comes the small fishing town of Porthleven.

The path continues along the cliff edge above Porthleven Sands to the shingle bank of Loe Bar, which encloses a freshwater lake, The Loe, one-and-a-quarter-miles long with wooded banks, and a national water-fowl reserve. The bar, a quarter-of-a-mile long and 600-feet wide, consists mainly of flints. An overflow channel has been con-structed to regulate the level and prevent flooding in the lower parts of Helston.

At Gunwalloe are two coves—the first Fishing Cove, the second Church Cove—separated by Halzephron Cliff. The church at the north end of the beach dates back to the thirteenth century. There are stories of shipwrecked treasure buried hereabouts, credible enough for searches to have been made, but nothing of real· value has ever been discovered. Round the next corner is Poldhu Cove with natural arch and large hotel. The cliff above is famous in the history of radio-communication. The Marconi Memorial marks one terminal of the first transatlantic wireless transmission in 1901; two decades later the first short-wave beam signals were transmitted from the same spot.

At Polurrian Cove (sands and large hotel) the schistose rocks 55 begin. Round the corner is Mullion Cove with small harbour, cave, arch, and Gull Rock pinnacle and Mullion Island offshore. Around are "lichen-covered cliffs, rocks piled on rocks, vaulted, tunnelled, ribbed and groined, with chasms and natural arches like the ruins of some vast cathedral".

We are now treading one of the outstanding pieces of Cornish coastline, in the words of Hockin, "scraped into fantastic pinnacles and precipices, torn into islands and ridges, and hollowed with caves and arches". The impressive Predannack Head has been used by rock climbers. This and other vantage points command widespread views over Mount's Bay. St. Michael's Mount stands out with Penzance and the coastline round to Tol-Pedn-Penwith. Inland is a sparse heathland landscape based on serpentine. On the coast path we pass on to serpentine once again over Pol Cornick and out to Vellan Head. Small quarries in Gew-graze were once worked for steatite (soapstone).

A few hundred yards farther on we reach an amphitheatre, known as Pigeon Ogo, which Folliott-Stokes describes as "the most dramatic arrangement of crag and precipice in Cornwall ... its perpendicular walls rise more than two hundred feet, and enclose in their sombre shadows a deep pool of troubled water, ever moaning and foaming in the caverns at their base. ... Beyond rises a strangely shaped peninsula known as 'The Horse'. Its crest is a jagged edge of rock fangs that

Lizard Point

defy the climber, while on either side it slopes perpendicularly to the sea." The path continues from these dizzying scenes along Kynance Cliff to the famous cove.

Kynance Cove is widely known and much visited (ten thousand sightseers daily in summer, it is said), so that special arrangements have been made to deal with the crowds. There is every justification for its popularity. The walker's remedy is the usual one—to come out of hours and enjoy at leisure an individual view of this picturesque scene: the pinnacles of Steeple Rock and Sugarloaf, Asparagus Island with its caves and blowholes, and the caves in the main cliff. Crossing Yellow Carn above Lion Rock, we traverse more cliffs of schist to Lizard Point and an abrupt turn to the east. Offshore the sea is peppered with reefs.

Ahead is the Lizard lighthouse, an important beacon for ships entering and leaving the English Channel. The first light, erected in the seventeenth century, was coal burning, but soon fell into disuse and was pulled down. The present edifice was constructed in 1756 and modernised in 1903. On the easterly corner of the Point is Lloyd's signal station which reports the passing of ships in these waters.

Lizard Town, half a mile inland, is a village with no more than car parks, cafés and curio shops which specialise in serpentine ware.

From the westerly corner of the Point the path rounds Polpeor and Polbream Coves. The lifeboat used to be kept here, the building and slipway remain, but it now operates from a more sheltered east-facing site in Kilcobben Cove by Landewednack. The next point, on which the lighthouse is built, has the isolated gabbro pinnacle of Bumble Rock at sea level. It is followed by Housel Bay, where there is a large funnel hole, known as the Lion's Den, formed by the collapse of a cave in 1847. After the headland of Pen Olver comes Belidden Cove and then Bass Point the site of the signal station. All round this area the paths are well-signposted and well-trodden.

The coastline now turns north, the well-marked path continuing along the edge of the cliff past Kilcobben and Church Coves and the Balk (with large daymark) close to Landewednack and on to Cadgwith, a tiny fishing village at the end of a narrow valley. On the southern headland is the highly impressive funnel hole called the Devil's Frying-pan which collapsed in 1868. This cliff has other caves below which can be approached only by boat; certainly the walker on the path sees none of them. However, the fine cliff scenery in schists and serpentine is adequate recompense. Three and a half miles away, across the bay, is the serpentine Black Head (70 metres/229 feet), the highest cliff on this side of the Lizard. The path reaches it by way of Polbream Point, the wide expanse of Kennack Sands and the gabbro headland of Carrick Lûz, where there is a camp.

Black Head is a minor turning point where the coastline, by now running east, turns north once again and we at last come into a view of the long south coast of the county. Chynhalls Point carries a promontory fort and a hotel. The path cuts across the base of the headland but there is a single track out to the farthest point. A hill leads down to Coverack.

Hereabouts, the coastal rock changes to gabbro. Close to the sea at Lowland Point is a flat area, a raised beach, at the foot of the former sloping cliffs. A mile on is Manacle Point with the dreaded Manacles reefs offshore, marked by a bell buoy and light and by sectoring of the flashes from St. Anthony Head lighthouse across the bay; marked also by day by the 30-metre (98-foot) spire of the church at St. Keverne just inland. Now we are approaching the Porthoustock quarry area. Just short of Manacle Point, south in fact of Dean Head, the path diverges from the coast inland to Rosenithon and then runs north-west across the base of Manacle Point to Porthoustock Cove. There is no reason to linger, but the cliff edge is again barred to the coastal walker, who must take tracks and lanes by Trenance to Porthallow Cove where he can join the sea once again.

This last small area of the peninsula, known as Meneage, is still relatively quiet and unspoilt. The scenery is gentle and the vegetation prolific. In another mile the Helford River, another fine example of a ria, is reached at Nare Point which is its southern portal. There is an extensive view to Rosemullion Head, across Falmouth Bay to Falmouth, St. Mawes and Zone Point and on up the coast towards Dodman Point.

The narrow inlet of Gillan Harbour can be waded at low tide, or a short diversion has to be made to the bridge at Carne. Dennis Head, fortified and captured during the Civil War, can be reached by a spur path, the long-distance route itself cutting across the base of the promontory. We continue westwards along the wooded shores of the river to Helford village and harbour.

Inland is Manaccan, which has given its name to manaccanite, an ore of the metal titanium, first found hereabouts. Half a mile west is Frenchman's Creek of the novel. Some miles farther west, towards Helston, one of the finest fogous is located at Halligye, close to the Elizabethan manor of Trelawarren.

We take the ferry across the river, once a haunt of smugglers, now famous for its sailing and oyster beds, and come to the Ferry Boat Inn at Helford Passage, thus entering the environs of Falmouth.

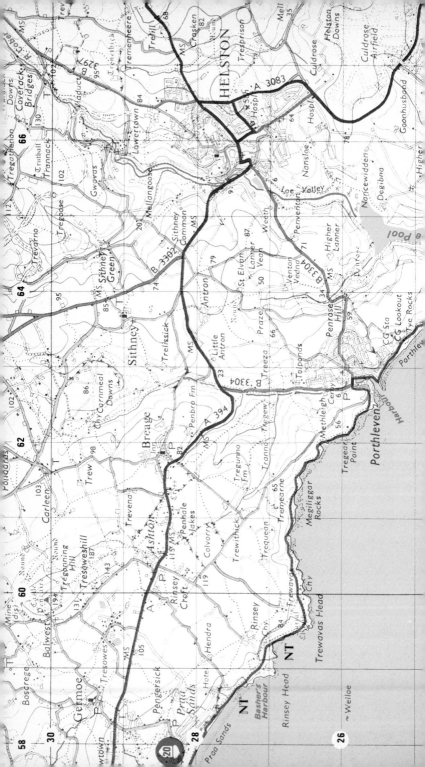

Helford River to Par

41 miles

The outstanding feature of this stretch of coastline is the extensive ria of Carrick Roads at Falmouth, the arms of which—Mylor and Restronguet Creeks and the Truro, Fal and Porthcuil Rivers—cut deeply back into the hinterland, with wooded banks mostly and easy slopes. The well-protected harbour of Falmouth, lying to the west of the Roads, has had a distinguished nautical history.

This coastline offers a wide range of experience, though apart from Falmouth there are no large towns. Some parts, such as the peninsulas of Roseland and Black Head between Mevagissey and St. Austell Bays, are well off the beaten track. There are some pleasant beaches, though except at Nare Head no very spectacular cliffs. Only one place, Mevagissey, a traditional Cornish fishing village-cum-tourist showpiece, really attracts visitors in large numbers.

Unfortunately this stretch also includes the most depressing industrial site on the county's coastline, the factory complex at Par where large-scale china-clay operations are always in progress. The china clay is mined around Hensbarrow Downs, inland beyond St. Austell; the spoil heaps produce the characteristic landscape known as the "Cornish Alps", prominent from as far away as the north coast.

The geological story is complex. We have returned now to the slates and shales of the Devonian around Falmouth and the rocks continue to be mainly slates for some distance onward. The headlands are usually of more resistant rocks, the coves of softer and there are numerous small beaches. Nare Head and the offshore islands and stacks, The Blouth, Jacka, Hartriza and Caragloose Points are all igneous; Greeb Point is volcanic ash; Black Head greenstone. Dodman Point on the other hand, which juts forth as prominently as any, is in fact of a grey slate and not particularly hard. It owes its defiant survival to being surrounded by deep water with little or no loose beach material lying around to effect erosion.

We start by the ferry across the Helford River. Later there are two more ferries, one of which poses a serious problem for the coastal walker. From Falmouth a scheduled service crosses Carrick Roads to St. Mawes. The ferryboat is sizeable and the trip delightful across waters teeming with shipping. The second leg across the Porthcuil River to Place is a different matter, for a ferry runs only during the summer months; at other times it may be possible to "hitch" a lift from a local or holiday boatman, otherwise the detour is considerable. 64 In fact, by the time the northbound walker rejoins the coast in the neighbourhood of Porthscatho he will probably decide to carry on and forget about the part he has missed. The southbound walker is in an even worse plight for he has to decide at Porthscatho whether to commit himself to going to Place at all. A reliable ferry at this point is an obvious necessity for a truly satisfactory long-distance route, so much so that the possibility of restoring it is being investigated.

Except for the urban areas of Falmouth and St. Mawes and, farther on, the industrial complex at Par, all this coast is Cornwall Area of Outstanding Natural Beauty. The National Trust owns several small properties around the Helford River, including Rosemullion Head; interior and coastline property amounting to half the area of the Roseland peninsulas; Pendower Beach by Veryan, Nare Head, Jacka Point near Portloe, Hemmick Beach, Dodman Point, Bodrugan's Leap by Chapel Point and Black Head. There are Youth Hostels at Falmouth (Pendennis Castle) and Boswinger by Dodman Point.

St. Anthony in Roseland lighthouse

On the northern slopes of the Helford River is the National Trust holding of Glendurgan; the house is not open, but on certain days of the year the very fine gardens are. The property also includes the beach and cottages at Durgan, through which the path from the Ferry Boat Inn at Helford Passage passes on its way along the north shore. Round Toll Point and below Mawnan we come on to Rose-mullion Head (also National Trust) from which we look back along the shore of Lizard to the Manacles and across Falmouth Bay to St. Anthony Head light. Within a mile comes Maen Porth beach with caves and arches. A short distance inland to the north-west are the fine sub-tropical gardens of Penjerrick, which are occasionally opened to the public. Now follows a succession of sandy beaches joined together by the made-up paths of urban Falmouth.

In 1539 Henry VIII began a systematic fortification of the harbours of the south coast of England by building a series of artillery forts at strategic and commanding points. The design was basically Italian; each had a centre citadel, surrounded by a ring of semi-circular casements, all looped for cannon. Two of the finest examples are here on each side of the Carrick Roads: Pendennis Castle on a promontory to the west, St. Mawes Castle facing it across the water. There is a road round Pendennis Point, where the castle is sited, and the path follows it all round the perimeter, full of interest because of the views it commands across the busy waterways. A hurrying traveller can, however, cross the neck direct to the harbour. At the end of the point is a cave 150-feet deep with a small passage at the end leading into the castle.

In Leland's day Falmouth was "the principal haven of all Britain". Defoe, who may well have been only copying, placed it next to Milford Haven as "the fairest and best road for shipping in the whole isle. . .". Its importance continued through the days of sail and it was a mail packet station up to the middle of the last century when the advent of steam led to the transfer of this function to Southampton. Falmouth continued to develop as a cargo port and then as a resort when the railway came. Beaches, waterways and sea cliffs provide a variety of entertainment for the visitor. Broad waters run north, deeply penetrating the countryside, to Truro and its cathedral.

A well-organised ferry takes us across, past Black Rock (with granite cone, iron standard and bell), to St. Mawes and the second artillery "castle", which has been described as "an architectural gem of the Tudor period". Here in St. Mawes they are so arrogant about their good weather, and one would imagine justifiably so, that a local hotel used to forgo its charges on any day when snow fell in the village. The whole of the peninsula between Carrick Roads and the sea is known as Roseland. The Porthcuil River divides it in half with St. Mawes on the westerly branch and our route onwards along the sea's edge on the easterly. The river must therefore be crossed from St. Mawes to Place Manor on the far side; but at the time of writing there is a ferry only during the summer months. At other times the traveller may be able to organise a private crossing, particularly as Place Manor opposite is now a hotel with its own transport needs. But there is no certain possibility. Otherwise it is necessary to follow A3078 northwards through St. Just Lane, and turn off right to 66 Gerrans and Porthscatho, the latter on the coast once again. It would

St. Mawes Castle

be unsatisfactory at this point to retrace one's steps in order to see the southernmost part of the peninsula.

We will assume, however, that we have managed to cross the Porthcuil River and arrived at Place. The path traverses the entire perimeter of Zone Point, passing St. Anthony Church (thirteenth century) and St. Anthony Head lighthouse on the way. Folliott-Stokes reports seeing as far as Dartmoor from the summit of the Point, certainly theoretically possible in conditions of exceptional visibility. And there is, of course, the grandstand view over the harbour and shipping lanes. The path continues now on the coast edge, running north-east past some small beaches to Porthscatho. The spire of the church at Gerrans serves as a daymark.

A considerable stretch of sand at Pendower Beach two miles ahead is reached by a straightforward path on undistinguished cliffs. Above the eastern end of this beach is a large round barrow close to the hamlet of Carne. According to legend a king was buried here with a golden boat and silver oars; unfortunately excavation has failed to turn legend into fact. Nearby there is an earthwork called Ring-arounds. Veryan, half a mile farther inland, has some curious round houses.

The path now runs out to the jutting promontory of Nare Head (101 metres/329 feet), with impressive exposures of igneous rock—in fact pillow lava. Gull Rock offshore has an outline almost Alpine with arêtes and pinnacles. The flat top of the head provides an elevated pathway and in two miles we come to Portloe by way of The Blouth and Manare Point. It is a tiny hamlet in a narrow cove. Dodman Point, which reaches out pier-like for almost a mile into the sea, looms ever higher ahead.

Two miles bring us to the Porthollands, West and East, both with small beaches and a few cottages. A straightforward cliff path leads on to Porthluney Cove, with sandy beach backed by the flamboyant ramparts of Caerhays Castle, which is John Nash "Gothick" constructed early in the nineteenth century on the site of an ancient castle. A cliff-edge path leads to Hemmick Beach (again sand) and on to Dodman Point which is 114 metres (372 feet) above sea level and topped by a tall granite cross which serves as a daymark. Traces remain of the ancient defences of the promontory in the shape of banks and ditches across the neck. The view is extensive: from Black Head on Lizard to Bolt Tail in South Devon—the limit of theoretical visibility—Eddystone lighthouse, the "Cornish Alps" and Bodmin Moor.

A conical hill, Maenease Point, shelters Gorran Haven on the south side; the path encircles it to the south and comes to the little fishing village with harbour and sands. Gwineas Rocks with bell buoy are a mile offshore. The path continues by the cliff round Chapel Point to the road at Portmellon, passing Bodrugan's Leap, a notable historic site. Here in 1485 Sir Henry Trenowth of Bodrugan, pursued by Sir Richard Edgecumbe of Cotehele, leapt his horse over (or down) the cliff (nearly 500 years of coastal erosion has made it impossible to locate the exact spot), to a boat waiting to take him to France. Edgecumbe consoled himself by taking over all Trenowth's possessions. The road runs over Stuckumb Point and down to the famous fishing village of Mevagissey.

Mevagissey—looking NE

"For narrow streets, quaint houses and appalling smells, Meva-gissey may be safely reckoned *facile princeps* in Cornwall", says Folliott-Stokes, writing some 70 years ago. Now it is a highly popular and much visited small resort, the usual facilities for dealing with tourists are well developed and there is a sand and shingle beach. Behind the trappings much of the atmosphere of an ancient Cornish fishing village remains, and the passing traveller will find it worthwhile to attempt to penetrate them. By Polstreath Beach and Penare Point the path comes to Pentewan Beach, where a detour alongside the road, away from the edge of the sea, is enforced by a gigantic caravan park, "the home of many wild flowers", so said a report of 70 years ago.

We cross the St. Austell River, the object of continuous pollution for a century and more. First it was the tailings from tin streaming and mining (Polzooth, three miles upstream, had 26 shafts working simultaneously at one time), later china-clay waste. Tin was also mined at the coast, the workings, as often, going out beneath the sea. Hereabouts were found the horns of an Irish elk, completely metallised by tin ore. Pentewan Stone quarried nearby is said to be a "famous" building material; it was certainly used at Antony House by Torpoint.

The next stretch of coast is one of those specially quiet and remote sections which we seem to come across from time to time. Indeed, though the path is scheduled to hug the coast all round Black Head and on into St. Austell Bay, at the time of writing arrangements were not complete and it may be necessary to follow a system of lanes and tracks some way inland. The path will cross the mouth of "the beautiful coombe of Hallane . . . a bosky natural theatre of greenery facing south and a regular sun trap". When it reaches Black Head it will open out a view across St. Austell Bay to Gribbin Head and its daymark by Fowey, and also into the bay and its industrial backdrop. Leland reported "vaynes of metalles, such as coper and other" on the cliffs, but they seem nevertheless to have escaped exploitation. Beyond Gerrans Head and Phoebe's Point we come to Porthpean, a sandy beach popular because of its proximity to St. Austell.

A straightforward path leads through Duporth to Charlestown, a small active china-clay port, constructed by, and named after, Charles Rashleigh in the eighteenth century. There are lock-gates to keep the ships afloat at low tide and the walker may perhaps (quite unofficially, of course) venture to cross them as a short cut. Otherwise he must pass round the head of the small basin. There is no incentive to linger.

Five-and-a-half-miles north-west lies the summit of Hensbarrow Downs (313 metres; 1,024 feet), the local granite massif, third in the line which starts with Dartmoor. The environs started as a mining area and were devastated in the usual manner. Then in the late eighteenth century deposits of china clay were discovered and wholesale development began. The material is excavated from pits and the waste, separated mainly by washing and filtering, is piled into huge mounds. Caraclaze, the oldest and largest pit, is 90 metres (294 feet) deep and a mile in circumference. Some pits, no longer used, are filled with water, forming striking lakes between the spoil heaps, which in places rise 100 metres (327 feet) above their surroundings. In spite of nature they stay predominantly white, "their tent-like stacks cresting the high moors as though an army of giants bivouacked there". From afar they loom on the horizon like snow mountains.

In this weird mixture of countrysides are two sites of interest to the walker. North of Hensbarrow summit, at Roche, is a massive granite outcrop surmounted by the ruins of a chapel haunted by the ghost of the giant Tregagle. It looks across the A30 to Castle an Dinas only three and a half miles away, from which it is only another half a dozen miles to the north coast of the county by Newquay.

To the west of the massif is the deep wooded valley of Luxulyan, spanned by the abandoned Treffys Viaduct, a granite structure on slender pillars, 200-metres (654-feet) long and 27-metres (88-feet) high, which once carried a railway, but is now used only by a leat and footpath. Nearby are some highly interesting large blocks, or boulders, of a type of granite known as luxulyanite containing large crystals of tourmaline. Here, according to Baddeley, is the largest block in Europe, measuring 49 feet × 27 feet with a 72-feet girth. These blocks are buried amongst luxuriant vegetation, but it is a very quiet locality in which to search for them. The church at Luxulyan village is said to be the finest granite church in Cornwall.

Now back to the coast. Beyond Charlestown is Crinnis Beach. At first the cliff top is covered by large houses and hotels, then, when these are left behind, the full glories of the china-clay manufactory fill the view. The path somehow finds its way through these places and comes to Par, a china-clay harbour with extensive sands alongside. The tide used to flow to St. Blazey Bridge, but the river gradually silted up because of tin streaming.

The only recommendable course for the walker is to pass from Duporth to Par Sands as rapidly as possible with some accompanying preoccupation to take his mind off the surroundings.

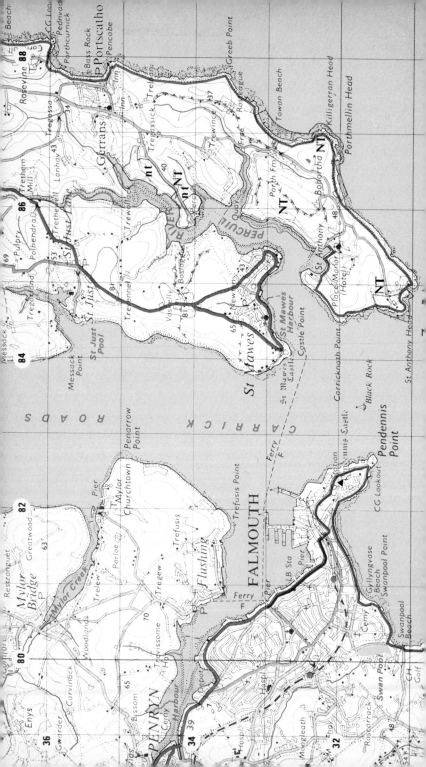

Par to Plymouth

37 miles

As we proceed along the southern coast of Cornwall towards Plymouth, the country becomes ever softer, more gentle and more built over. There are no sizeable towns until Plymouth, which, of course, is beyond our boundaries. Fowey and Looe have small urban areas but there is no interruption of the path. The only place likely to be crowded is the most widely known of all Cornish fishing villages, Polperro, second only to Land's End as a goal for pilgrims; and it is adequately developed to deal with them. The path might well have been dislocated by the forts around the harbour at Plymouth, relics of the days when it was a great Naval port needing land-based defences to command the approach channels. But, in fact, only Tregantle Fort enforces a detour away from the sea and even then can be passed on the beach at low water.

There are three more rias, a small one at Looe, one of medium size at Fowey and an extensive one at Plymouth, where several important rivers join in a common mouth. The Tamar, as we have seen, rises near Marsland Mouth on the north coast, and marks for most of its length the county border with Devon. It is joined by the Tavy from Dartmoor above the Victorian rail- and modern road-bridge at Saltash. From the west from Bodmin Moor comes the Lynher River and the three rivers together form the Naval anchorage of the Hamoaze, from which a narrow channel between Mount Edgcumbe and Stonehouse leads out into the Sound. Cremyll Ferry across these narrows marks the end of the path, where we cross out of Cornwall. There is a regular ferry service here, as also on the only other crossing in this section, that between Fowey and Polruan across the Fowey River.

The rocks exposed in this stretch of coastline are nearly all Dartmouth Slates of the Devonian, notable for their wide range of colouring: "Indian red and green tints predominate", "pink, purple and green", "from off-white and a bilious yellow to warm Devon red, purple and black", are typical descriptions by various observers. The resistance of the headlands to erosion by the sea is often the result of bands of harder rock or strata hardened by folding. At Rame Head for example the slate is hardened by bands of grit veined with quartz.

From Gribbin Head almost to Looe is Cornwall Area of Outstanding Natural Beauty; the remaining part, for reasons which are fairly obvious, is not. The National Trust owns five miles of coast round Gribbin Head, St. Saviour's Point and other properties around Fowey Harbour; an extensive holding at Lantic Bay; parts of Lantivet Bay including the cliff below Lansallos; one mile of coast west of Polperro; Bodigga Cliff and foreshore beside Millendraeth Beach and Trethill Cliff; and Sharrow Point and Higher Tregantle Cliffs above Whitesand Bay. Mount Edgcumbe beside Plymouth Sound is now a Country Park.

Eddystone lighthouse, nine miles off Rame Head, provides a distant landmark for most of the way, but there are no mainland lights between St. Anthony's Head by Falmouth and Start Point far away in South Devon.

This section gives interesting and varied going in the earlier stages. From Polruan to Polperro is a fine secluded cliff line; from Polperro to Looe the path is well marked and scenic. After Looe, however, the presence of Plymouth begins to be felt with holiday houses, chalets and caravans in the coves and on the tops of the cliffs. Many of the headlands jut boldly seawards with fine views up and down the coast.

There are Youth Hostels at Golant by Fowey and in Plymouth just beyond the end of the Cornwall Coast Path.

We can now turn our backs at last on the grimness of Par and set out southwards along the coastline of Gribbin Head. Soon comes the fishing village of Polkerris, "in a little cove so completely surrounded by a crescent-shaped hill that it resembles the stage and pit of a natural theatre". The public house is so well ornamented that it has been likened to a museum. The walker will come across many similar pubs elsewhere along the path.

Gribbin Head (74 metres/242 feet) reaches out half a mile in advance of the general cliff line to the east and thus commands a fine view in that direction. Dodman Point opens up once again beyond Black Head to the west, while eastwards rise the South Cornish headlands to Rame Head, with Bolt Tail in South Devon way beyond. There is a daymark here, 25-metres (82-feet) high, erected by Trinity House in the 1830s. Turning the seaward end we pass Polridmouth Cove, with "almost sub-tropical flora", where there is a grotto lined with minerals and crystals. At the entrance to the haven are the few remains of St. Catherine's Castle, another of Henry VIII's coastal defence forts. Nearby rises the Rashleigh Mausoleum.

There is now a fine view over the ria of Fowey River. Carew's words hold good today: "In passing along, your eyes shall be called away from guiding your feet, to descry by their farthest kenning the vast ocean sprinkled with ships that continually this way trade forth and back to most quarters of the world." It was customary many years ago, in time of war, to close the harbour with a chain drawn between the blockhouses on either side of the channel. We pass Readymoney Cove and come to Fowey.

Above the town are quays from which china clay is exported. The river, which rises on Bodmin Moor close to Brown Willy, offers a wide channel all the way up to Lostwithiel and walkers may care to diverge that far in order to see Restormel Castle, a good example of the so-called shell-keep construction, where the summit of the primitive mound, originally defended by circular wooden palisades, was reinforced in the course of time by a circular stone curtain wall. A mile beyond the castle is Lanhydrock House, the gardens of which are occasionally opened. Only two and a half miles from Fowey, just

Mouth of the Fowey River

west of Golant, is a hill-top camp, Castle Dore, with two ramparts and ditches with an outer diameter of 420 feet. Opposite Golant to the north-east of St. Veep is a curious linear earthwork, known as Giant's Hedge, traces of which appear at other places farther east as far as Looe. Its function, possibly defensive, possibly as a boundary marker, is unclear.

We cross by the regular ferry service to Polruan, which has a single street sloping down steeply to the harbour. The path takes us all round the headland, past the National Trust's St. Saviour's Point and up to Blackbottle Cliff (120 metres/393 feet) from which we look out over Fowey towards the multiple white cones of Hensbarrow. The coastline is in view from Rame Head to Dodman Point with a glimpse of Lizard's Black Head opening up beyond.

Between here and the National Trust holding of Chapel Cliff at Polperro lies a little-used and relatively inaccessible series of cliffs. The summits are high but the cliff faces are not precipitous. We round Lantic Bay to Pencarrow Head, a blunt promontory which the path follows round. The hills behind reach almost 140 metres (450 feet). Then follows Lantivet Bay, wider and more open with some sandy

coves and sloping cliffs behind; Palace Cove once had a quay. The
dangerous reef of Udder Rock is marked by a bell buoy and a white
beacon on the cliffs above. There is a descent to sea level at West
Coombe in the middle of the bay, followed by a climb to Lansallos
Head at around 140 metres (450 feet). Once again the fronting face is
far from precipitous. Another descent to sea level at East Coombe is
followed by a similar cliff line towards Polperro.

Suddenly we reach National Trust land, and a well-developed set
of footpaths on Chapel Cliff below Hard Head leads us inexorably
into Polperro. For the general visitor this is the paragon of all
Cornish fishing villages, much visited and photographed. Cars and
coaches are confined to parks high up the valley and visitors have to
walk down. Every ingenuity is employed for their entertainment. "It
is so commercialised", says Burton, "that it has forgotten how to be
natural; every door sports a pisky knocker and every house has a
smugglers' den." The village is sited in a steep-sided cleft between
125-metre (400-foot) hills, the houses are jumbled together willy-nilly;
"quaint old houses, quaint old porches, immense chimneys, outside
stairs, narrow streets and a bisecting stream".

The tiny harbour has an entrance narrow enough to be closed by baulks of timber in rough weather. It is sheltered on the seaward side by a 30-metre (100-foot) headland called the Peak. It is said that in the great storm of 1817 the tides swept over its highest point, "as near as the eye could judge at double the height of the rock, not in mere spray but in a solid body of water". This must have been quite outstandingly impressive, viewed from a safe distance, though wave statistics would seem to indicate that this report is somewhat exaggerated. At Pelynt, two miles to the north, is a barrow cemetery with ten bowl barrows.

Between Polperro and Looe the path is well maintained and signposted. We round Downend Point and come to Talland Bay, noteworthy for its beautifully coloured slate rocks. A caravan site overlooks the beach. Between a pair of black-and-white painted beacons on the cliffs above Polperro and a similar pair on the east headland of this bay is the "Measured Mile" used for speed trials by the Admiralty. Beyond Hore Stone Head (105 metres/343 feet) is Portnadler Bay with the once-inhabited Looe Island offshore. The path comes eventually to a made-up road close to Hannafore Point, on which we walk to West Looe.

Looe comprises the small towns of West and East Looe, joined by a bridge which spans the combined streams of the West and East Looe Rivers. It is still an important fishing port with narrow, winding streets; there also are sands. This is the centre of the Cornish big game—shark—fishing activities, now grown into an important tourist attraction.

The West Looe flows past many miles of wooded banks. The Giant's Hedge earthwork, which we saw at St. Veep by Fowey, is detectable here also, close to the river. Between the two rivers near Duloe is a 37-foot-diameter stone circle, unusual in that it is constructed of quartz blocks.

Because of recent cliff falls the path no longer climbs to the cliff from the east end of the beach at East Looe. Instead it runs through the town from a point near the bridge and crosses the shoulder of the hill, past houses and bungalows, on to the seaward face of the cliff. Straightforward trackway leads now to Millendraeth Beach, the site of a village of chalets and holiday caravans.

The path will continue eventually to hug the cliff edge. Parallel to it inland are a few hundred yards of excellent roadway, the purpose of which in this particular location is entirely obscure; this links with the coast road to Seaton which has to be followed at present. Hereabouts, at Murrayton, there is an unusual zoo housing a collection of Brazilian woolly monkeys. The path comes down along a tree-covered cliff to Seaton Beach (sand and pebbles), where there is a holiday camp. Folliott-Stokes had to take to the beach between Millendraeth and Seaton Beaches: " . . . slate cliffs, a jungle of bracken, ivy-clad pinnacles, elder and fruit bushes".

This is the mouth of the Seaton River, which rises a dozen miles to the north on the slopes of the isolated Caradon Hill (370 metres/ 1,210 feet), an outlier of the easterly part of Bodmin Moor. There are numerous antiquities around: Trevethy Stone, the remains of a chambered tomb, King Doniert's Stone and a stone circle, the Hurlers.

The Cheesewring, believed at one time to be the work of ancient man, is a grotesque granite tor with typical outline resulting from weathering. The tors in this part of the moor, which culminates in Kilmar Tor (395 metres/1,292 feet), are very reminiscent of Dartmoor. Years ago when the high lighthouse was operating on Lundy, it is said that this point commanded a simultaneous view of that lighthouse and the other at Eddystone more than 80 miles to the south.

A guide-book writer early in the last century, who has to be commended for penetrating even this far, said of the next section of the coast that, "it gives a romantic ride particularly from Looe to Mount Edgcumbe when sea, promontories, rocks and precipices, combine to form a terrible sublimity". Today its reputation falls well below these brave words; the cliffs are gently sloping for the most part and do not bear comparison with most others in the county, while the coves and even the tops of the cliffs are built over.

The path hardly succeeds in escaping from the coast road as we pass through Downderry, then when the road turns inland to avoid the steeper slopes of Battern Cliff we strike off once again into comparative wilderness. Vegetation-covered slopes lead up to open cliff top on Battern Cliff (141 metres/461 feet), the highest cliff on the southern coast of Cornwall. The road is soon back close on our left and has to be followed at present. It is hoped the route will eventually avoid having to use it for the next one and a half miles, before finally sloping down to the village of Portwrinkle at the edge of the sea.

On the golf course to the east of Portwrinkle is a good example of a medieval pigeon-cote, or calver house. The path keeps close to the edge of the sea for a short distance, but is finally forced to make an inland detour east of Crafthole, to run parallel to the road in order to circumvent Tregantle Fort (disused) and a series of rifle ranges. To avoid this inland excursion it is possible, when the tide is right, to take to the beach below, called Long Sands. However, there might be hazards even here if firing were in progress. We rejoin the cliff edge at Tregantle Down.

The next stretch, towards Rame Head, is dotted with bungalows, shacks and caravans. This coast is the south side of a peninsula, much of it less than two miles wide, bounded on the north by the Lynher River. Looking down on the river is Antony House, built in the early eighteenth century, belonging to the National Trust and open to the public. On the opposite bank, at Trematon, is another shell-keep type medieval castle. Nearby is St. John's lake wild-life site.

Rame Head, with camp and ruins of a chapel dedicated to St. Michael, juts far into the sea. Nine miles away, somewhat west of south, is the famous Eddystone lighthouse marking a dangerous reef, the graveyard of many a Plymouth vessel. The present tower, the fourth on this site, was erected by Douglass in 1882. The first, built by Winstanley and one of the earliest deep-sea lighthouses in the world, was destroyed in a storm in 1703. The second, the work of Rudyard, lasted 50 years before being destroyed by fire; the third, built by Smeaton, lasted until threatened by changes in the reef itself. It was then moved block by block to Plymouth where it now stands on the Hoe looking out towards its successor 14 miles away.

The route is now straightforward. It is one and a half miles to Penlee Point, western portal of Plymouth Sound, and another mile to Kingsand and Cawsand, typical twin fishing villages which have 81 missed the over-popularity of better-known places farther west. Mount Edgcumbe, closed until recently to the coastwise walker, is now a Country Park owned jointly by Cornwall and Plymouth and the path follows the water's edge all round its wooded slopes. This was the estate coveted in 1588 by the Duke of Medina-Sidonia, High Admiral of the Spanish Armada. The route used to cross the hill above by way of Maker Church; this way is still available to anyone looking for a last small piece of quiet countryside.

And so we come to Cremyll Ferry and the end of the Cornwall Coast Path. Stonehouse is only a few hundred yards away and there is a regular service. There has been a ferry here, once the main route into Cornwall, for some 600 years. Celia Fiennes crossed by rowing boat: "I was at least an hour going over, almost a mile, and notwithstanding there was five men rowing and I set my men to row also, I do believe we made not a step of way for almost a quarter of an hour, but blessed be God, I came safely over at last."

The ferry boat takes us over into Devon.

Polperro

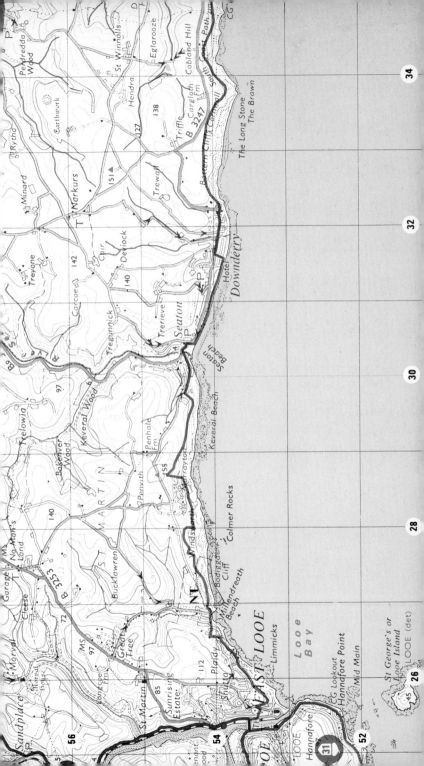

The sea and the coast

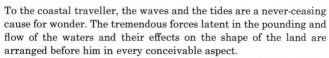

To the coastal traveller, the waves and the tides are a never-ceasing cause for wonder. The tremendous forces latent in the pounding and flow of the waters and their effects on the shape of the land are arranged before him in every conceivable aspect.

A full study of tidal behaviour is beyond the scope of this book (see bibliography). The chief tide-maker is the gravitational attraction of the moon which produces high tides on the surface of the earth approximately beneath it, and similar tides simultaneously on the far side of the earth. The moon rotates round the earth once a day, but the earth itself is rotating on its axis in the same direction so that the period of the tide averages about 12 hours 25 minutes (in fact other factors cause it to vary between 12 hours 11 minutes and 12 hours 35 minutes). The moon's path is elliptical, producing greater effects the nearer it approaches the earth: variations of +22 per cent to −16 per cent from the average.

The sun also has an effect on the tides, amounting to rather less than half that of the moon. When sun and moon act together we have specially high tides, called spring tides; in between, when they oppose, occur the markedly lower neap tides. The path of the earth round the sun is also elliptical, causing tides to be highest in winter, when we are nearest to the sun.

The behaviour of the simple earth tide is of course much modified by surrounding land masses. Thus, in Cornwall, the actual tidal wave travels in an opposite direction to the earth tide. High water occurs at Land's End some 45 minutes ahead of that at Plymouth and 66 minutes ahead of that at Bude. The tidal range (the vertical distance between high and low water marks) in Cornwall varies between 10 and 16 feet.

Knowledge of the heights and times of the tides is essential for the walker who ventures below high water mark. This information is displayed prominently in many resorts or can be worked out beforehand using an almanac. But no problem will arise if the path be strictly kept to at all times.

The patterns of the waves on the surface of the sea also fascinate. There are two principal sources of waves: swell, or waves of considerable wavelength which originate from a distant disturbance; and waves raised by the wind blowing across a sea otherwise still. With the second type the height of the waves is related to the distance over which the wind has blown (the fetch); this is why the waves are higher and more spectacular in the far west facing out across the

Atlantic Ocean in the direction of the predominating wind. There are many stories about the periodicity of waves above average height. On a purely statistical basis this random system will produce one wave in 23 which is twice the average and one in 1,175 that is three times the average.

As the waves reach shallower water the drag of the sea bed causes their velocity to diminish, but the number of waves in a given time remains the same, so that the waves get closer together. The water tends to pile up until the waves become unstable and "break", either by the top sliding down the forward slope (spilling) or overtaking the next trough (plunging).

The coastwise walker sees every phase of the moulding of the land by the sea, the results depending broadly on the type and stratification of the rocks and the direction of the incoming waves. The processes now in train were set in motion originally by a change in the relative level of the sea and the land. When a river valley with tributaries is thus invaded, the resulting scenic feature is a drowned river valley, known as a ria; there are many examples in Cornwall: the estuaries of the Camel, Gannel, Fal, Fowey, Looe and Tamar Rivers. Occasionally there are examples of even earlier relative movements of land and sea in the form of raised beaches, such as between St. Ives and Morvah, and Lowland Point on the Lizard.

When incoming waves break on the shore a mass of water, called the swash, runs up the beach until its energy is expended; then it flows back to the sea again—the backwash. The swash hurls sand and shingle up the beach, the backwash carries some material back towards the sea on sand beaches, but filters back through the stones

Bude, looking north

on a pebble beach. Thus pebble beaches tend to become steeper, while mixed beaches become sorted, with the larger material at the top.

When there are fewer than about six waves a minute the whole process is unhindered, swash and backwash are separate, material is cast up on to the beach, and the waves are said to be constructive. When there are more than six waves a minute the backwash begins to interfere with the swash, the build-up lessens until finally there is a net loss of material; the waves are now said to be destructive.

When waves beat on an inclined land face, material is removed and a notch formed which continues to deepen because of abrasion by sea-borne material: the beginning of a cliff. Eventually the un-supported layers above collapse, falling into the sea to provide more materials for the abrasion process. The cliff becomes higher, while at the same time developing a wave-cut platform at its foot. This is either bare rock or covered with sand and shingle which absorbs more and more of the energy of the wave attack as it widens, and thus helps to protect the cliff behind.

The type of cliff which results depends on the nature of the rocks and their dip. When the strata slope inwards the cliff will be steep, when outwards the upper strata slide over the lower and tend to produce areas of landslip. When cliff-forming rocks are prominently jointed, both vertically and horizontally, as, for example, granite, or where there are veins of softer material, narrow inlets (called "zawns" hereabouts) or caves are often formed. The collapse of a cave at the inland end, hastened perhaps by hammer blows from air trapped by the incoming waters, produces a funnel hole, of which there are many Cornish examples. The collapsed material is washed away by the sea to produce the spectacular results we see today. At an earlier stage, if there is, perhaps, a small hole only at the landward end, the pressure exerted by the water in the narrowing cave ejects some of it at the hole, hence a blowhole.

When waves approach an indented shoreline they lap round head-lands which are thus attacked from the sides. The action tends to emphasise the form of a promontory; softer strata where they occur are taken out altogether. First a cave is hollowed out on either side, they join to form an arch, then finally the roof of the arch collapses, producing a stack or pinnacle.

When waves approach a beach obliquely the swash runs obliquely up the slope, while the backwash runs straight down it. There is a tendency therefore to move material sideways along the beach, re-sulting in a general movement along the coastline, the so-called longshore drift. This sort of process accounts for the accumulation of bars or banks of sand or shingle at river mouths, such as the Doom Bar at Padstow and the Loe Bar.

In some places the headlands are of harder rocks than the bays be-tween, in others they are local rocks simply hardened by folding or mechanically by veins of more resistant rock types. In any case the headlands bear the brunt of the major erosion by the sea; they tend to be worn away and to be deposited in the bays between, so that the final result is likely to be a relatively straight coastline. The Cornish coast is far from this condition at present.

The big dune areas are produced when the prevailing winds from the sea blow large amounts of seaside sand inland. Movement and incursion of sand are controlled nowadays by the planting of appropriate vegetation. Previously the uncontrolled drifting of sand buried buildings and even legendary cities. Sometimes a particularly violent storm will remove all the sand from a cove, leaving shingle or the bare rock; such situations usually revert in the more normal days that follow, but long-period fluctuations between rock and sand are sometimes observed.

The spectacular interplay of the forces of nature and their effects on the edge of the land will be with the walker along every step of his journey.

Rough seas at Gurnard's Head

Geology, rocks and mining

The rocks of Cornwall divide into three broad groups. The first consists of a considerable area of sedimentary rocks (mostly sandstones, shales and grits of the Devonian and Carboniferous periods) stretching from coast to coast, often locally hardened by heat or pressure into slaty rocks, known in this part of the world as "killas". Penetrating this mass is a series of granite bosses; four of which—Bodmin Moor, Hensbarrow Downs, Carnmenellis and the West Penwith moors—are in Cornwall; the others are Dartmoor and the Isles of Scilly. Finally the Lizard Peninsula is made from entirely different and more ancient rocks, igneous and metamorphosed, having no clear relation to the remainder of the county.

The sedimentary rocks were first laid down beneath the primeval ocean, where they compacted and hardened. Then in the Devonian period dykes and sills of an igneous rock, greenstone, were injected among the strata. Violent earth movements associated with the Armorican folding of Permo-Carboniferous times thrust these rocks towards the nearly immovable block of Wales; the strata were further hardened and folded into the fantastic patterns we see now, for example, in the cliffs between Marsland Mouth and Dizzard Point. The whole formed a huge anticline with Devonian rocks on either side sandwiching the newer Carboniferous beds which appear at the coast to the north of Boscastle.

In Carboniferous times masses of magma were injected from below, baking the surrounding rocks into killas. The magma did not break the surface at this time, but cooled slowly beneath it, so that the granite-forming minerals—felspar, quartz and mica—separated out in large crystals, while other more volatile materials, liquid or gaseous, formed the metalliferous ores eventually exposed by mining operations. In places carbonic acid converted the felspar to kaolinite, the future basis of the china-clay industry.

Subsequent erosion by weather and water stripped off the upper layers and exposed the granite. The whole mass sank beneath the sea, from which it emerged progressively in stages, each stage producing a characteristic flat platform at the prevailing sea level, which can be traced at various points throughout the county. Thus the 430-foot platform, which was formed around 12 million years ago, can be clearly seen between St. Ives and Morvah. Another relative change of level even more recently produced the succession of rias which nowadays are an outstanding feature of the Cornish scene.

Ore-bearing rocks are found in a series round the injected granite

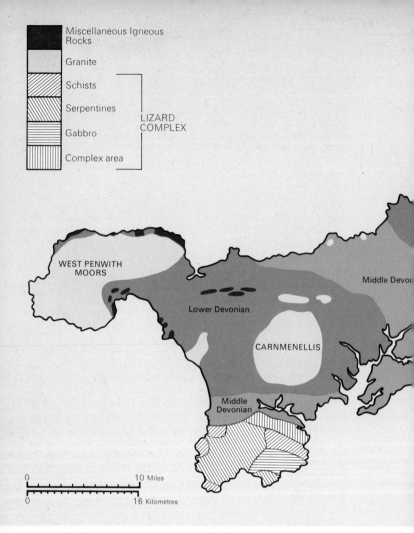

Miscellaneous Igneous Rocks

Granite

Schists

Serpentines

Gabbro

Complex area

LIZARD COMPLEX

WEST PENWITH MOORS

Middle Devon

Lower Devonian

CARNMENELLIS

Middle Devonian

0   10 Miles

0   16 Kilometres

masses, differentiated by their various temperatures of freezing. Deepest are tin and tungsten minerals, then copper, nickel, cobalt and arsenic, followed by zinc and lead and finally iron. This explains why certain mines, dug originally for copper, could be worked at a later date for tin by sinking the shafts to a lower level. All mining has taken place therefore close to the boundaries between the injected granite and the killas, into which the lodes spread as they sprouted from the molten magma.

Cornwall has been a source of metals for thousands of years, and was probably the site of the legendary Cassiterides, visited by

Phoenician merchants in search of tin over 3,000 years ago. First the

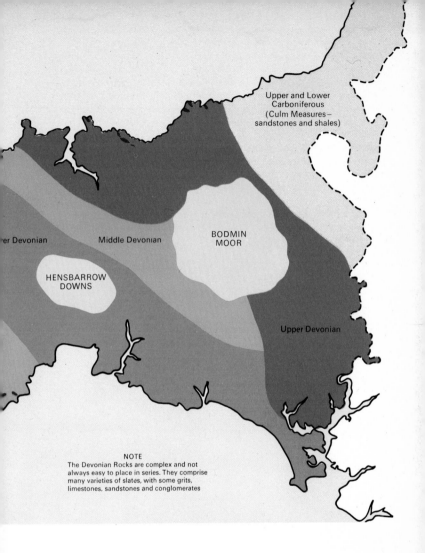

Upper and Lower
Carboniferous
(Culm Measures—
sandstones and shales)

...er Devonian

Middle Devonian

BODMIN
MOOR

HENSBARROW
DOWNS

Upper Devonian

NOTE
The Devonian Rocks are complex and not
always easy to place in series. They comprise
many varieties of slates, with some grits,
limestones, sandstones and conglomerates

metal was obtained from the surface by streaming, that is by washing out the heavier ore from lighter materials collected from stream beds or below sea cliffs. Later it was extracted from lodes at ground level or from near the surface by the use of heat or crude explosives. Shaft mining began much later and thenceforward the problem became increasingly one of removing water from workings in order to be able to penetrate to greater depths. Many miles of drainage tunnels, or adits, were bored; man-power, horse- and water-power were all utilised for pumping. Then finally came the steam engine.

First in the field, early in the eighteenth century, was the Newcomen engine, followed some 50 years later by the markedly more 95 efficient Watt engine. Soon there were engine houses everywhere with their attendant chimney stacks, whose ruins are part of the characteristic landscape of today.

From the mid-eighteenth to the mid-nineteenth century copper was more important than tin; indeed in the middle of this period Cornwall was the chief world source of copper. However, other, more easily accessible sources were found, so that by 1865 tin was again in the ascendency. Deeper digging in the copper mines revealed tin at a lower level, and the mines started into a new activity. Again foreign sources gradually took over, so that after 1918 the industry declined rapidly. By 1945 only two mines were in operation: Geevor near Pendeen lighthouse and South Crofty by Camborne. Throughout recent years the price of tin has continued to rise, so that the possibility of its economic mining in Cornwall is once again under consideration. Certain mines have made a fresh start, notably the great Levant mine, next door to Geevor, where the original workings went out under the sea. When the mine was abandoned the sea broke in and it was a herculean task to seal the breach before workings could be driven through from Geevor. Users of the path must look with some disquiet on developments of this sort.

The Cheesewring

Cornish Alps—china-clay workings

Contorted strata at Millook Haven, Bude

97

The rocks of Lizard belong to a much earlier geological period. They are all—serpentine, schists, gabbro and Lizard granite— fundamentally igneous rocks which have welled up from lower levels. The schists are the metamorphosed remains of the very earliest rocks, some igneous, some sedimentary, modified by the successive injections of the others. There is a fertile soil below the schists which form the impressively steep sea cliffs. The serpentine, which probably came next, underlies an infertile soil given over to heathland. The carving and polishing of this rock for use as ornaments has become a local tourist-orientated industry. The dark-coloured igneous rock, gabbro, provides fine fertile soil and is also quarried for road metal. Lastly there is granite, very different from that of the main granite bosses of Cornwall; it is of a pink colour and not prominently cleaved horizontally or vertically, and so does not produce tors or castellated cliffs. These rock types account for the great variety of scenery which the walker meets on the path round the peninsula.

Collecting pebbles on beaches has always been a popular pastime and continues to hold interest even today. The careful searcher can, it is said, find samples of semi-precious stones, notably amethyst, citrine, chalcedony, agate, carnelian and jasper. It may well be true, and Marazion is a site frequently recommended. However, sea-polished specimens of the ordinary rocks and minerals of the county, pebbles which show the junction of different rock types, pebbles of mineral ores where the sea has eroded lodes on the cliff face, are all worthy of hunting.

The mining areas are of great interest to the collector: first, for specimens of mineral ores, second, for the possibility of finding single crystals of various mineral substances. Minerals usually crystallise in a conglomerate mass of very small crystals due to the crystallisation process starting more or less simultaneously at a large number of points throughout the mass, but under special conditions, where crystallisation spreads from only one point, an ordered structure results—a so-called single crystal of the substance in question. The form and colour are characteristic of the material—a beautiful geometrical pattern. In mining days most good single crystal specimens found their way into museums and collections, and they can be seen in profusion, for example, at Penzance, Truro and Camborne Museums. The spoil heaps are thus unlikely to have been a very good source in the first place and they have been searched extensively by enthusiasts. Discoveries are most likely to be made in mine passages or on cliff or quarry faces, all of which need a careful and circumspect approach.

The imprint of man on the coast

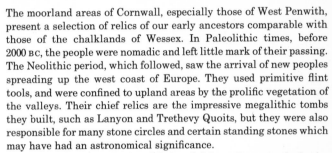

The moorland areas of Cornwall, especially those of West Penwith, present a selection of relics of our early ancestors comparable with those of the chalklands of Wessex. In Paleolithic times, before 2000 BC, the people were nomadic and left little mark of their passing. The Neolithic period, which followed, saw the arrival of new peoples spreading up the west coast of Europe. They used primitive flint tools, and were confined to upland areas by the prolific vegetation of the valleys. Their chief relics are the impressive megalithic tombs they built, such as Lanyon and Trethevy Quoits, but they were also responsible for many stone circles and certain standing stones which may have had an astronomical significance.

Around 2000 BC the Beaker folk invaded from the east—the beginning of the Bronze Age. A certain amount of settled farming was practised, resulting in the enclosure of some small fields at high levels. These enclosures are still to be seen and, close by, the fragmentary remains of the hut circles in which these people lived. The presence of minerals also contributed to this culture. Bronze Age burial mounds, the round barrows, are still prominently upstanding in many places, for example at Carne by Veryan and Trevelgue Head at Newquay. The Bronze Age cemetery at Harlyn Bay is an outstanding antiquity.

About 350 BC new invaders brought the Iron Age. They built the many hill-top and promontory forts as protection against the native inhabitants, also finding them useful against later arrivals. Since rock was plentiful the walls were often constructed from this material. The promontory forts were purely defensive and never permanently inhabited, but hill-top forts often contain dwelling sites also. There are examples of the former at Rame Head, Dodman Point, Castle Kenidjack, Rumps Point and the Willaparks and of the latter at Trencrom Hill, Castle an Dinas (both types) and Chûn Castle. Most Iron Age people lived in villages outside the defensive works; the best example is at Chysauster by Gulval, Penzance. They constructed lynchets to improve cultivation. The setting aside of small fields, demarcated by walls made from the on-lying rocks, was a notable feature of their culture—the pattern is retained today in places on the West Penwith moors. The winning of tin by streaming flourished.

The coming of the Romans, and the Dark Ages which followed their 99 departure some 500 years later, had little significance for this corner of England.

We estimate the size and importance of English ports in medieval times by examination of the statistics of ships contributed to King Edward III for the siege of Calais. Fowey sent 47, the largest number from any port in England except Yarmouth; while London provided 25, Plymouth sent 26 and Looe 20. Centuries later the ships which congregated hereabouts to oppose the Spanish Armada came from the same places in much the same sort of proportion. The easily defended havens of the ria coastline, the natural harbours, had been developed first; later many small coves at the end of lesser river valleys became small settlements under the protection of the flanking headlands. Where nature herself did not provide a sheltered anchorage for boats, man added quays, sea walls and breakwaters.

All these ports, each having its own tiny fleet of vessels, supported an ever-expanding fishing industry. This served local needs at first, being particularly important because of the comparative infertility of the inland soil; later the advent of the railway helped to extend the market to places farther away. In the heyday of the industry odd boats operated from the sands of even the tiniest of coves (for example Porthzennor Cove near Gurnard's Head). For years pilchards were the basis of Cornish fisheries; arriving in huge shoals, they were trapped close to the shore in seine nets, the operations directed by observers, called huers, on the headlands above. Huers' houses, in which they sheltered, still exist at Newquay, St. Ives, Sennen Cove and Cadgwith. The scale of catch was enormous. Figures for a record day's catch of pilchards have been put at 12 million, even as high as

Lanyon Quoit

100

75 million. Much of the catch was salted and exported to Italy and Spain. The industry nowadays is only a shadow of what it was in those far-off days. Suddenly, for reasons unknown, the pilchards found Cornish waters no longer attractive.

Deep-sea fishing by drifters was also carried on for a wide variety of catch, now only a few active fishing ports, such as Newlyn, remain, though small-scale operations continue to meet local and holiday needs. Other ports grew up for the export of tin, copper and china clay. Falmouth is the only substantial cargo port.

A sea-going people, earning a living from the sea, takes active steps to protect its mariners from the dangers they must face and to guide them safely to port. Some very early coal-burning lighthouses were constructed, for example, on the Island at St. Ives and Lizard Point. Later, shore-based lighthouses were sited strategically down the coasts, while ocean lights were set up sometimes in the face of quite incredible difficulties on reefs like Eddystone, Wolf Rock and Longships. All carry powerful foghorns which provide another characteristic background to sea-coast experience. Lesser reefs have whistling or bell buoys (an eerie accompaniment to a coast walk on a fine day) or are aligned by markers on the land. A host of other prominent features, obelisks, church towers and such-like structures complete the network. These are the daymarks which, lacking a light, signal their warnings only in daylight hours.

Nevertheless wrecks occurred, and still do, sometimes quite unaccountably. For most of us, wrecks have a morbid fascination and the literature that has grown up around them is prolific. Needless to say the lifeboat service is well organised. Most boats can be looked over for a small voluntary payment. One of the most interesting features of a wreck is to witness the marvels achieved by salvage methods which look crude but turn out to be surprisingly effective.

The deliberate causing of wrecks, of luring ships on to the rocks by displaying misleading lights on land, was a charge levelled at the local population in years gone by. There is a wealth of legend and little knowledge of how much of this is actual fact. Undoubtedly when wrecks did happen the impoverished local people quickly removed everything of value, but there is not much evidence that they committed murder to further their ends.

As mining exploration spread over the countryside the worthwhile lodes were followed wherever they happened to go. Sometimes they finished on cliff faces, or were followed for miles out to sea, by tunnels cut into the sea bed. The coastline therefore underwent an apparently arbitrary despoliation, which is in fact concentrated where the metamorphosed rocks around the various granite masses come close to the sea. Mine works and mine shafts litter the landscape. In addition lengthy adits were dug taking water from the mines and draining it to the sea. Man has certainly left his mark on the countryside in the mining areas, the most notable coast locations being St. Agnes and St. Just.

Quarrying for road metal has also devastated some coastal areas, notably the Penlee Quarry by Newlyn and the large workings at Porthoustock. Fortunately there are no china-clay workings immediately adjacent to the sea.

At the end of the eighteenth century smuggling was already a well-

Mullion Cove

established custom, and indeed had the status of an eminently re-
spectable business. The government imposed such high duty charges
that it became worthwhile, in a sense almost, one might say, an
irresistible challenge, to remove dutiable goods from the prying eyes
of the authorities. In its heyday smuggling involved almost all the
community to a greater or lesser extent, with law and order repre-
sented by only a few Naval and Revenue officials. In some places the
smugglers behaved much as they pleased.

It was smuggling that led to the founding in 1822 of the Coastguard
Service. Coastguards, many of them ex-Naval men, patrolled by boat
or on foot along the cliffs, in a continuous check of coastal happen-
ings, embarkations and landings. The coastguard path along the
cliffs ran much as does our present-day recreational coast path, close
enough to the edge to command a view of every part of the shore. It
has been suggested that the existence of the coastguard path implies
the moral existence of a right of way at the sea's edge which should
now be seized for use by the public. But this is a naïve view, for the
right of way has undoubtedly gone, in some cases beyond recall.

Cottages for coastguards were built in seaside places large and
small. These characteristic buildings seldom have an official function
nowadays, are either deserted because of remoteness and lack of
roads or used as holiday cottages. Coastguard look-outs crown prominent headlands all along the coast—simple buildings with a big
sweep of windows on the seaward side. Most are no longer in use,

though they could apparently still be manned if required.

The coming of the railway to Cornwall in the mid-nineteenth century enabled goods to be exported more readily to the rest of England. In the opposite direction it brought the rising tide of holiday-makers, who now form the major industry of the county. Little ports developed their beaches; remote bays, coves and sandy shores sprang into holiday-enhancing life. The great days of the *Cornish Riviera Express* and the *Atlantic Coast Express*, romantic symbols of a cheap and highly efficient railway system, were about to begin. When the motor-car arrived it opened up every country lane leading to every cove, no matter how small or secluded. Visitors began to seek a change from the conventional hotel or boarding-house holiday, in favour of greater mobility and the offer of "bed and breakfast" in ordinary houses, cottages and farmhouses; holiday chalets were erected for summer visitors only and rows of garish caravans filled many a field. Thus the facilities which promote the enjoyment of the countryside tend inevitably to destroy the very features which were the attraction in the first place.

The coastline offers an extensive range of recreational activities, some of which require specialised knowledge from those who engage in them. *Walking:* the whole reason for the path's existence; often combined with outdoor nature studies. *Rock climbing:* the subject of a short note (page 110). *Caving:* practised in a small way by enthusiasts who explore mine shafts and adits in a countryside where 103 there are no natural caves of any considerable size. *Sailing* (also *canoeing*): popular pastimes in the wide expanses of the big rias; *ocean sailing* too gives interesting opportunities of exploring islands such as the Scillies. *Sea angling*: always popular, while *big game fishing*—sharks—attracts an ever-increasing following. *Swimming*: an essential element of any Cornish holiday, but it is important to pay serious heed to warning notices, flags and the like, which strike a necessary note of caution in some of the waters around this dangerous coast. *Surfing*: available on many beaches facing the long fetch of the Atlantic Ocean. *Underwater swimming* and *marine archaeology*: both pastimes have many devotees and many interesting and exciting finds have been made within the last decade.

Mid-twentieth-century man is still unable to control the despoliation of the countryside. One thinks of the radar dishes at Cleave and Goonhilly, the chemical complex at Nancekuke, the increased industrialisation of Hayle and Par, the over-running by sheer weight of numbers of beauty spots such as Land's End, Polperro and Kynance Cove, the traffic congestion in the narrow streets of many a town and village, acre upon acre of chalets, caravans and tents. By now the walker can no longer use the roads to go safely and pleasantly from place to place, so that the provision and maintenance of an adequate network of footpaths has become imperative.

We must halt the motor-car short of the coast and persuade visitors to walk the last few hundred yards to the edge of the sea.

Shipwreck

Wild life

No account in a book of this length can possibly deal adequately with any of the many aspects of nature likely to be encountered along cliff and shoreline. At every step of the way, the observant walker will have cause to marvel at nature's infinite diversity of life and form. Birds, animals, insects, plants and shore life can all offer studies of quite staggering complexity; even to sketch in their background, however etiolated, would take more space than can be accommodated here.

The walker with little or no naturalist knowledge will enhance his experience if he can but recognise some of the most common specimens. Among booklets for the beginner are: *Birds of Cornwall, Shells on Cornwall's Beaches* and *Flowers of the Cornish Coast* (see bibliography at end of guide). For the more expert there is additional information to be gained from manuals such as: *Wildlife in Cornwall, Wild Flowers in Cornwall, Birds of the Cornish Coast* and *An Introduction to the Seashore Life of Cornwall and Scilly* (see bibliography).

Through the County Naturalists' Trust, or through specialised scientific bodies, it is possible to meet local experts in one's own field. There are also museums, aquaria and an extensive literature in the form of journals and so on.

Among the various travellers who have described the Cornish coast in literature are some who devote considerable space to observations of nature. Folliott-Stokes, for one, has many an evocative passage to describe the wild flowers he saw on his journeys over the whole length of the county. To quote a typical passage:

"Files of stately foxgloves line the stone hedges," he wrote, "stand like sentinels at every stile, and climb the hill in whole battalions. The wayward honeysuckle loads the air with its rich aroma. The spidery tentacles of the predatory dodder cover themselves with a network of crinkled bloom. Thousands of blue scabious star the walls, and the round-leaved pennywort crowns them with its tall spikes of pale greenish white flowers. The tender yellow stars of the silver-weed and the creeping cinquefoil line the lanes, and the wax-like bells of the cross-leaved heath are to be found on moor and cliff. The grass is cushioned with masses of fragrant thyme, and starred with centaury, and the blue, white and purple blossoms of the milkwort. Here and there the giant mullein rears its stately column of yellow bloom. . . ."

1 Herring Gull. 2 Great Black-backed Gull. 3 Kittiwake. 4 Spring Squill. 5 Burnet
Rose. 6 Common Scurvy Grass

7 Shag. 8 Razorbill. 9 Common Guillemot. 10 Wild Carrot. 11 Sea Pink (Thrift).
12 Mesembryanthemum (Hottentot Fig)

Weather

We are beset on every side by weather forecasts—television, radio, newspapers, the prognostications of local experts—the traveller has numerous sources of information. He may even carry his own radio. Unfortunately, as frequently pointed out, the weather in the far west often arrives ahead of the forecast.

The shipping forecasts, which are the most informative, divide the western seas into areas: Lundy from Minehead to Land's End and Plymouth from Land's End to Start Point. Farther out the source of future weather will most likely be in Finistère, Sole, Fastnet or Shannon. Visibility is indicated in these forecasts as follows: 0. Dense Fog (50 yds.), 1. Thick Fog ($\frac{1}{10}$ mile), 2. Fog ($\frac{1}{4}$ mile), 3. Moderate Fog ($\frac{1}{2}$ mile), 4. Very Poor Visibility (1 mile), 5. Poor Visibility (2 miles), 6. Moderate Visibility (5 miles), 7. Good Visibility (10 miles), 8. Very Good Visibility (30 miles), 9. Excellent Visibility (above 30 miles). Unfortunately good visibility often indicates incipient bad weather.

Some people become remarkably adept at weather forecasting, others have absolutely no idea, however long they may have lived locally; the traveller's problem, which appears insoluble, is to decide which type he is talking to. A useful rule is given by Watts in *Instant Weather Forecasting* (Adlard Coles, 1968)—the crossed winds rule: "Stand with your back to the lower winds, or the direction of motion of lower clouds, then if the upper winds or clouds come from the left the weather will deteriorate, if from the right it will improve, if parallel then no marked change is likely."

Warnings of gales are passed to mariners by the hoisting of storm cones in prominent places on land: point up for a northerly gale, down for a southerly. When the storm cones are out the walker on the path can expect some spectacular seas, furious pounding of the shore by waves larger than usual, driving spray high up the cliff faces and over harbour walls and quays, spume whipped from the sea driving horizontally along the tops of the cliffs. When he has seen enough he can turn inland away from the alien sea and all becomes endurable once again.

Average winter temperatures are higher in the west than in the east of England and it is unusual for snow to fall, nor will it stay around long if it does. The annual rainfall, somewhat higher than that of southern or eastern England, is not excessive, that of the south Cornish coast being rather higher than that of the north. These conditions encourage the growth of sub-tropical vegetation in sheltered sites such as Penzance, Falmouth and many other places inland.

The Country Code

Guard against all risk of fire

Fasten all gates

Keep dogs under proper control

Keep to the paths across farm land

Avoid damaging fences, hedges and walls

Leave no litter

Safeguard water supplies

Protect wild life, wild plants and trees

Go carefully on country roads

Respect the life of the countryside

Rock climbing

The last two decades have witnessed a remarkable advance in the status of the West Country, and Cornwall especially, as a centre for rock climbing. Activity is confined almost entirely to sea cliffs, and walkers on the path may be able to watch climbers in action, or even do some climbing themselves (few will be able to resist the odd scramble met here and there). But a word of caution here. Rock climbing can be dangerous and should never be embarked on by anyone who has not had experience of this highly attractive pastime.

Though one or two pioneer alpinists are known to have visited the county and to have stretched their legs upon the rocks, the first serious campaign was mounted by Arthur Andrews, who arrived on the scene about 1880 and finally moved to Tregerthen by Zennor around the time of the first world war. He had been a pioneer rock climber in North Wales. Here he found much the same kind of sport, but the presence of the sea posed additional problems: difficulties of approach and retreat; climbers cut off for the period of the tide; backgrounds as potentially savage as those of mountains, yet much more varied. Andrews conceived and developed the cliff-foot traverse: a horizontal climb between easy ways down the cliffs, which not only demanded climbing skill, but provided these other exhilarating features also.

It took Andrews a lifetime to see his vision take hold among climbers. He showed his climbs to his friends, wrote about them in climbing journals; he persuaded the Climbers' Club to set up a headquarters at Bosigran in West Penwith and helped to write a climbers' guide-book to the cliffs, published in 1950. Slowly interest grew as more and more climbers of high ability went west to climb beside, and out of, the sea. The great face below Bosigran Head, the cliffs of Land's End, Pordenack Point, Carn Lês Boel and Chair Ladder were climbed by increasingly difficult ways.

The exploration spread to other parts of the county. First to the Hartland Point–Widemouth Sands coastline, where some of the great slabs and pinnacles were ascended. Then, later, climbs of very high standard were made at Pentire Point, St. Agnes Head and Tintagel Head, while a determined attack was made on the many sea stacks, such as the Merope Islands by Padstow and Long Island near Bossiney Haven.

Maybe there are not many who will wish to follow in the steps of the super-experts, but every walker, as soon as he puts his hands on the rocks for balance, should take note that he is making a humble start on rock climbing. Who knows whether he will wish to go further?

General information

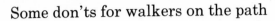

Some don'ts for walkers on the path

Don't—go near the cliff edge unless you are sure that it is not
crumbling or overhanging
—go near the cliff edge unless you are sure you have a "head
for heights"
—set out on a beach traverse on a rising tide
—set out on a beach traverse unless you have a firm goal in
mind and are quite sure you can reach it in the time available
—embark on activities involving rock scrambling (use of the
hands) or rock climbing unless you have already had rock
climbing experience

Signs of distress at sea

Rocket, parachute flare or hand flare showing red light.
Rockets or shells throwing red stars one at a time at short intervals.
Smoke signals with orange-coloured smoke.
Any signalling method reproducing the Morse letters SOS
(———···———) or the word "Mayday".
Human figure slowly and repeatedly raising and lowering out-
stretched arms.
Continuous sounding of any fog-signalling apparatus.
Flames on a vessel from a burning tar barrel.
International code signal of distress NC (blue and white chequered
flag with 16 squares above a flag striped horizontally—blue, white,
red, white, blue).
A square flag with a ball below it.
Red ensign upside down.
Red ensign made fast in the upper part of the rigging.
Coat or article of clothing on an oar (small boats).

The walker who sees any of the above should dial 999 at the earliest
opportunity and inform the coastguard. In addition there are the
obvious signs of trouble, such as ships listing or on fire, small boats
capsized, aeroplanes in the sea, airmen dropping by parachute or
people in the water. All the above information is displayed prominently all along the coastline on poster CG22, issued by the Depart-
ment of Trade.

Book list

Early works on Cornwall (all reprinted within the last two decades) by: Carew, R.; Defoe, D.; Fiennes, Celia; Leland, J.; Lysons, D. and S.; Norden, J.

Balchin, W. G. V. *Cornwall*. The making of the English landscape series. Hodder and Stoughton. 1954.

Barton, R. M. *An Introduction to the Geology of Cornwall*. Bradford Barton, Truro. 1964.

Beer, R. *Wildlife in Cornwall*. Bradford Barton, Truro.

Burton, S. H. *The Coasts of Cornwall*. Werner Laurie. 1955.

Folliott-Stokes, A. G. *The Cornish Coast and Moors*. Paul. n.d.

Gresswell, R. K. *Beaches and Coastlines*. Hulton Educational Press. 1957.

Hamilton Jenkin, A. K. *The Cornish Miner*. David and Charles. 1974.

Harper, C. G. *The Cornish Coast—North. The Cornish Coast—South*. Chapman and Hall. 1910.

Hockin, J. R. A. *Walking in Cornwall*. Methuen. 1944.

Noall, C. *Cornish Lights and Shipwrecks. Cornish Seines and Seiners. Smuggling in Cornwall*. Bradford Barton, Truro.

Noall, C. and Farr, G. *Wreck and Rescue round the Cornish Coast* (3 vols). Bradford Barton, Truro.

Page, J. L. W. *The North Coast of Cornwall*. Hemmons. 1897.

Paton, J. A. *Wild Flowers in Cornwall*. Bradford Barton, Truro.

Penhallurick, R. D. *Birds of the Cornish Coast*. Bradford Barton, Truro.

Pilkington, R. *The Ways of the Sea*. Routledge and Kegan Paul. 1957.

Pyatt, E. C. *Coastal Paths of the South West*. David and Charles. 1971.

Rogers, C. *A Collector's Guide to Minerals, Rocks and Gemstones in Cornwall and Devon*. Bradford Barton, Truro. 1968.

Salmon, A. L. *The Cornish Coast*. Fisher Unwin. 1912.

Tricker, R. A. R. *Bores, Breakers, Waves and Wakes*. Mills and Boon. 1964.

Turk, Stella M. *An Introduction to the Seashore Life of Cornwall and Scilly*. Bradford Barton, Truro.

Woolf, C. *An Introduction to the Archaeology of Cornwall*. Bradford Barton, Truro.

Booklets (Tor Mark Press, Truro):
Shells on Cornwall's Beaches. Flowers of the Cornish Coast. Birds of Cornwall. Cornwall's Structure and Scenery. The Pebbles on Cornwall's Beaches. Cornwall's Old Mines. Sea Fishing in Cornwall. Antiquities of the Cornish Countryside. Cornwall's Ports and Harbours. The Story of Cornwall's Lifeboats. Industrial Archaeology of Cornwall.